Computer P
CO

Melinda Fisher's introduction to computing came at the Meteoro-
logical Office, where she was a member of the numerical forecasting
research team. After further research work she gained commercial
programming experience with an insurance company, a computer
bureau and British Rail before joining ICL Training as a lecturer in
1977. She is now Manager of Application Training, responsible for a
team of forty lecturers covering the ICL machine range, and has
travelled the world as a lecturer and programming consultant.

TEACH YOURSELF BOOKS

Computer Programming in COBOL

Melinda Fisher

TEACH YOURSELF BOOKS
Hodder and Stoughton

First printed 1982
Fourth impression 1986

Illustrated by G. Hartfield Illustrators

Copyright © 1982
Melinda Fisher

ISBN 0 340 20383 8

Phototypeset by Western Printing Services Ltd, Bristol. Printed and bound in Great Britain for Hodder and Stoughton Educational, a division of Hodder and Stoughton Ltd, Mill Road, Dunton Green, Sevenoaks, Kent, by Richard Clay (The Chaucer Press) Ltd, Bungay, Suffolk

Contents

1

General Introduction

This book is designed to enable you to learn how to program a computer using a language called COBOL.

It would be helpful, although not essential, if you had some computer concepts' appreciation or can use another language, like BASIC.

Chapter 2 introduces you to the important elements of computer hardware and the way that a computer can be programmed. This chapter also introduces you to the role of a programmer in a commercial installation. The way that programs must first be planned using flowcharts is described before introducing you to the COBOL language in chapter 3.

A simple program is described in chapter 4. A complete but simple piece of logic, this illustrates a COBOL program before you learn all the features of the language. Chapters 5–11 describe in detail the commonly used elements of the language, and include data description and two types of data file, as well as printing reports. Chapter 12 introduces the advanced features of the language, including modular programs.

Writing the COBOL code is not enough to produce a working program. Chapter 13 describes the process of developing a written program, and chapter 14 contains full documentation of an example program. The example program takes you through the program specification, the logic design, the written code and the tested program. Chapter 15 describes some of the applications that COBOL programs can be used for, and overviews a batch and real-time system.

There are four appendices for you to reference; they should be constantly used. COBOL is too complex to remember in detail, so it is essential that you check your work and reference the appendices if you need confirmation of detail.

COBOL is an acronym for Common Business Oriented Language; it is in common use throughout the world in business organisations. The business applications tend to be long and complex, often dealing with large amounts of data. This leads to large and complex computer systems. This book contains exercises and examples that have business applications but because realistic programs are large the exercises are scaled down to a manageable size.

Appendix 4 gives the exercise solutions. Most of the chapters have exercises. You should do each exercise, re-reading the text if you have problems. Having completed the exercises check your solutions with those given in Appendix 4. There is often more than one correct solution, and so in some cases alternatives will be stated. It is essential that you understand fully the solutions, and can see why yours differ, before proceeding with the next chapter. You should not skip a chapter as the facilities taught in one chapter are used in the next.

2

Introduction to Data Processing

It is important that you understand some of the basic computer concepts before you learn to write a computer program. This chapter introduces you to data processing, describes the role of a programmer and how to design the logic of your programs.

Data processing is a modern technology and is becoming an important part of commercial and business life. Data processing is simply the manipulation of information to produce useful results. As far back as the fifth century the abacus was in use. It was the first machine designed for counting and is in fact a primitive computer. It was the advances in electronics that enabled data processing to develop to its present state. Today's technology enables data to be manipulated at very high speed; it is reliable and the results produced are not prone to human error in the way that those produced by a manual system are. Other great benefits of modern computers are that they enable huge quantities of data to be stored in a small amount of space, and they allow fast access to that data.

Hardware

The computer itself is called *hardware*. Let us look at the components of a computer.

Store

The central piece of hardware is the computer store, often called *memory*. Store is made up of millions of pockets, each capable of holding a character of information. This character is represented by 8 bits (a *bit* is the smallest unit of store). A bit is capable of holding the value 0 or 1. There are 256 different patterns that 8 bits can form:

therefore there are 256 different possible characters represented by a computer. (Chapter 5 explains this in more detail.) This capability of each bit to hold two values, 0 or 1, leads us to name the number system *binary*.

Processor

This next piece of hardware is also central to the computer. The *processor* is the 'work horse' of a computer – it does all the work. It manipulates information which is held in the computer's store; does arithmetic on stored data; and controls other parts of the computer. It is the power of the processor that determines the power of the computer.

Peripherals

Initially, the computer store is empty and there must be a means of placing information – inputting data – into store. The devices used to input and output data are called peripherals as they are on the periphery of the central pieces of hardware – the store and processor.

There are two groups of peripherals: the slow or basic peripherals, and the fast magnetic peripherals.

Slow peripherals

CARD READER

The card reader is the most common input slow peripheral. Punched cards are 80 columns wide, capable of holding up to 80 characters of information. Holes are punched in each column and different formats of punched holes represent different characters. The most common characters, 0–9, are represented by a single hole, A–Z are represented by two holes, in different patterns.

The information on the card is read and the data passed to the computer's store for processing.

LINE PRINTER

The line printer is the most common output slow peripheral. Continuous stationery and a fast moving print head produce lines of print with the appropriate vertical and horizontal spacing.

The information printed will be held in the computer's store and output onto hard copy, i.e. the line printer.

Fast peripherals

MAGNETIC TAPE

Magnetic tape is an inexpensive way of holding large volumes of data. A magnetic tape looks like a large reel of tape recorder tape. The principle is the same – the magnetic tape is magnetised to form patterns and each pattern represents a different character. Unlike the tape recorder, the magnetic patterns are not played back to produce sounds but pieces of data that can be read into the computer's store for processing. The magnetic tape drive has recording and playback heads and is therefore termed an input-output peripheral. Data can be stored on the tape and input to the computer. Data in the computer's store can be recorded on the magnetic tape and stored. Computer installations may have hundreds of magnetic tapes, each tape holding large amounts of information or *files* of data.

DISCS

Magnetic discs are a more expensive but more flexible way of storing large volumes of data. Discs, as the word suggests, are like a stack of long player records on a central spindle. Each disc platter has two surfaces and the surfaces have a series of concentric tracks. The tracks can be magnetised in the same way as magnetic tape. The disc pack can consist of many platters, it is placed on the disc drive which has a *read/write* head for each surface. This head does not have a stylus, like a record player, but hovers above the tracks. It reads data encoded magnetically in the tracks and can record data on the tracks, hence the term read/write. The advantage of a disc is that the heads can move to any of the tracks on a platter and read or write data. The magnetic disc head has the ability to move to the piece of data directly, and allows for the data to be accessed *randomly*. Random access means that data can be read or written in an irregular order, i.e. no particular sequence. Magnetic tape only allows for data to be accessed in the sequence that it is held on the tape. There is an analogy to the tape recorder and the long playing record. To get to a track on a tape you have to wind the tape, passing the early tracks and positioning the recording heads at the correct place. With a long playing record you can place the stylus straight on to the selected track. The magnetic tape is accessed sequentially; the magnetic disc can be accessed randomly or sequentially. The terms 'sequential access' and 'random access' will be used again later in this book.

VIDEO TERMINAL

There is another peripheral that is becoming more widely used: the video terminal. This is a keyboard (like a typewriter) and a screen (like a television). When a key is touched it causes a character to be displayed on the screen. A complete line can be formed and sent to the computer's store as data. Data residing in store can be displayed to the screen. So the video terminal is an input-output device; it allows the user or programmer to communicate with the computer.

Fig. 1 shows a computer with a selection of peripherals. This computer has two magnetic tape drives; magnetic tape can be input or output to a computer but cannot be both at the same time. There is one card reader which is input and a line printer which is output. The magnetic disc can be input and output at the same time, as can the video terminal. A typical computer will have many discs, video terminals and magnetic tape drives, it may also have more than one line printer and card reader.

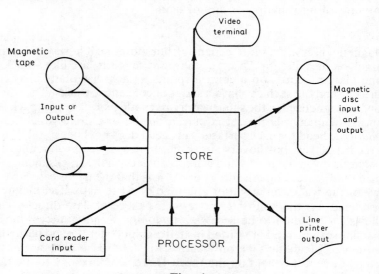

Fig. 1
A computer with a selection of peripherals

Software

The peripherals are fundamental to the use we make of a computer, enabling us to input and output data.

Input, process, output is the pattern of all computer applications. It is also the pattern of most manual systems, e.g. take an order, pack goods, invoice the goods, send goods. The computer is given the instructions to process the input in order to produce the results. These instructions are held in the computer's memory or store. A group of instructions designed to fulfil a particular function is called a program. A program only resides in the computer's store while the data is being processed. This enables the computer to be programmed to do many different things. The program is stored on a magnetic tape or disc when it is not being used. Programs are known collectively as computer *software*.

There are many types of software:

- Applications programs, the sort of program that you will learn to write in this book, are programs that are made to measure for a particular user or function.
- Utilities are programs that are general purpose, e.g. to sort data into sequence, to print the content of a data file. These are usually supplied by the computer manufacturer.
- Program development software, to create data files, compile and correct programs. This is described in detail in chapter 14.
- Operating systems are programs that help the operator to do his job, they help to maximise the computer's resources. An operating system can allocate peripherals and computer store so that programs can run. It interacts with programs, e.g. by handling program error messages. It can keep a record of what happens to a program and when it was run. This is called a log or monitor file. Operating systems are machine-dependent and can be very simple or very complex. They all help to handle the computer's workload.

Programs

The computer's store is made up of pockets, each capable of holding an 8 bit binary pattern. These binary patterns can represent data which has been input or is to be output to peripherals. The binary patterns can also represent machine understood instructions, known as *machine code*. A machine code instruction instructs the computer, e.g. it can add the contents of two data fields together, it can move the content of a data field to another field, it can request that a data record be input or output.

BEFORE

Address	7016	7017	7018
Content	6	1	4

Address	8121	8122	8123
Content	1	2	4

AFTER

Address	7016	7017	7018
Content	6	1	4

Address	8121	8122	8123
Content	7	3	8

The pockets of store in a computer are numbered, enabling each pocket to be referenced. We call this reference the *address*. A data field, three characters long, may start in store address 7016: it will occupy the storage area from address 7016–7018. The three pockets of store may each contain a binary pattern representing numeric data, say the value 614. There is another three character field starting at address 8121, this field contains the value 124. A machine code instruction can, say, add the contents of the three character field starting in address 7016 to the contents of the field starting in address 8121. The result will be the value 738 in address 8121–8123. The instructions themselves have an address because they occupy store. This set of instructions with its associated data areas is called a *program*.

Files, records, fields
Data is processed by a program; this is only possible because data is organised and presented in a predetermined format. Data is stored in *files*. A file consists of *records*. A record consists of one or more pieces of information known as *fields*.

A filing cabinet holds record cards, say one record card for each customer of the company. Each record card consists of three fields: the customer's account number on the top left hand corner, the customer's name at the top right hand corner, and the customer's address in the middle of the card. When a record is accessed, the filing clerk knows that on the top right hand part of the card the customer's name can be found. It is the same with a computer program. A program can read one record from a file at a time. The data in the record is in a fixed format and the program can describe this for the computer. It says that the account number is first and will be 6 digits long, followed by the name of 20 characters, then the address of 60 characters. If the filing clerk has arranged the record cards in account number sequence we can say that the records are sorted into a particular sequence.

The filing clerk can access the data, one card at a time, starting at the first and finishing with the last record card. This is possible with computer files and is called *sequential processing*, all peripherals can support sequential files.

If the filing clerk wants to access one particular account number card it is possible to go to that card directly. This is called *random access* and computer files can be accessed randomly. Only disc files can support randomly accessed files.

The role of the programmer

Although you may be learning COBOL simply as an interest, it is important for those considering a career in programming to appreciate the task of a programmer in a commercial installation.

This book's primary task is to teach you COBOL, the syntax, and how to code a program.

It would be easy to believe that a programmer coded all day, but this is far from the truth. The programmer's role is a comprehensive and responsible one.

It is advisable for you, the programmer, to be familiar with the computer system with which you are going to work. It would be impossible to understand the complex business functions being processed by the system, but an overview of the system's input, processing and output should be possible.

A diagram of the program and suite interfaces is usually presented using a system diagram.

The first task is to read and understand the program specification. This is the document that defines the program input, processes and output. These specifications are sometimes ambiguous but it is you, the programmer, who clarifies these ambiguities with the *system designer*. It is essential that you make no assumptions, as they may have repercussions at a later date.

Having read and fully understood the program specification, the next stage is to design the logical steps needed to meet the specification accurately. This logic design takes a diagrammatic form as a flowchart or structure diagram. Flowcharting is the method used in this book and is described in this chapter. Having designed and drawn the flowchart it is important that you 'prove it'. This is called *dry running* and is used at many stages in the development of a program. To dry run a flowchart, create a sample of input data which is simple and caters for all known conditions, e.g. if there is an account number of six digits just use a single digit. Write this data out – it will be useful later – and also write out the results that you would expect from this data if it were accurately processed.

Imagine that you are the computer obeying each flowcharted instruction, process each piece of data and note the results as you go. When all the data has been dry run, check your results with the expected results. If they disagree amend the flowchart and dry run the data again. If the results agree then your logic is correct. A sound logic diagram now will save you many headaches later. Make sure the diagram is neat and readable.

Now you can code your logic. It is important to write clearly and neatly on alternate lines of the coding sheets; this allows for amendments to the coding. Data names and procedure names should be meaningful and there should be ample comment lines.

When you have completed your coding, dry run it. In the same way as you did with the logic, you must now check your code. Use the same data. It helps to have a colleague obeying each instruction, thus ensuring an unbiased assessment of the code. If the results do not match those expected, correct the code and dry run again. If the results agree then the coding is ready for data preparation.

There are a number of ways of preparing your coded program for the computer. The traditional method is punched cards, where each line of coding is encoded on to a punched card. The other methods are key to disc and key to tape systems – these are cheaper and quicker than the card system and enable the prepared data, on disc or tape, to be read directly into the computer at high speed. We will assume the use of cards.

You have already designed your outline test data for dry running, now you must prepare detailed test data for testing your program on the computer. Where possible use data that is realistic; the person who wrote the specification should be able to help you. When designing the test data ensure that all conditions and combinations of conditions have been catered for. Ensure that the volume of data is enough to test things like more than one page of output to a report file. It is unlikely that your test data can match the volume of data normal for production running – fifty to a hundred test records should be enough. There is software available that can help you generate test data in larger volumes.

Having prepared the test data, you must prepare the detailed 'expected results'. Take each test record and prepare the results that should be output from your program. Both the test data and the expected results form an important part of your final program documentation. You will use the results to check against the computer output from your test runs. The test data can now be sent for data preparation. Your program has been punched on to cards. The program source, which is what we call your punched program cards, must be in the same strict sequence as the coding that you wrote originally. Be careful not to drop the cards!

The program source is now ready for compilation. The *compiler* is a piece of software that reads your program source and checks it for syntax errors. (*Syntax* is the rules or 'grammar' of the language.) The compiler lists your program source with sequence numbers and also a list of errors found during compilation. The sequence numbers are used to reference the erroneous lines. The compiler also produces *object code* (code which can be understood by the computer).

Initially we are more interested in the errors. The compilation listing should be examined and each error located and corrected. Correction of the program errors is done by using another piece of software, the *editor*. The editor allows you to change lines of code, insert lines and delete lines. Inevitably you will make mistakes, and using an editor is the simplest method of correcting them.

Besides correcting errors, the compilation listing gives you another opportunity to dry run your program. The neatly produced computer listing is easy to read. Check carefully for missing full stops: check your file descriptions as well. The compiler can only detect syntax errors *not* logic errors.

Having prepared your corrections and had them punched on to cards, you are ready to compile your program again. Before compiling you must edit it to correct the errors. The editor corrects your program character by character, line by line, and it produces a corrected version of your program. It is this corrected version which is compiled.

The compiler will again produce a listing and if there are still errors, an error list. You continue with the process of editing and compiling until there are no errors: we call this a *clean compilation*. When the program is clean you are interested in the object code produced by the compiler – without this object code your program cannot be run or executed on the computer.

The next stage in program development is testing.

You now have the test data punched and have created the test input file or files to your program, you also have the expected results.

The compiler has produced object code which is loaded into the computer and executed. Your program will read your test data and process it according to your COBOL coding. It will produce output. If the output is to a disc file or magnetic tape file the content of the output file can be printed.

You now carefully check the computer output with the expected results. You note each discrepancy and examine the latest compilation listing to find the relevant piece of code with the logic error. This detecting of errors is called 'debugging'. When you have found every error you continue with the process of editing, compiling and testing.

Eventually your program is completely correct: it is 'program tested'. This does not mean that your job is over. The program must go through rigorous trials.

The program is *suite tested*. This usually involves small amounts of data being processed by each program in the suite. The first program will be run and the output file from that program will be input to the next program, and so on. If the suite testing is successful it will prove that the programs interface or link together correctly.

System testing uses a realistic production volume of data which is processed by each program in each suite. This proves that the suites interface and that the total system produces the output that the user wants. During either of these tests you may have to change your program, either because your program is wrong, or the program has to be changed because of new processing requirements.

If the latter is so you have to correct, recompile and retest your program. This might mean changing the test data.

Finally your program, along with other programs in the system, will go into production.

You should complete your program documentation for production handover. The documentation consists of the program specification, approved specification amendments, the flowchart, the compilation listing, list of test data, the expected results and the actual results and, if necessary, a written explanation of what the program does. This documentation will help any programmer to maintain your program in the future. If your program fails or needs enhancing in years to come and it has been badly written or documented it will be very difficult to correct.

Logic design

Before the COBOL language is learned it is important that the programmer can design accurate logic. Many jobs demand that things are planned before they are implemented. Designing logic is the programmer's planning stage, when he draws a *flowchart*.

The flowchart describes in detail the sequence of events and the processes within each event. The flowchart must be an accurate diagram of what is needed to write a program described by the program specification. This sequence and the detailed processes can then easily be written in the COBOL language.

When flowcharting you should use the following symbols. The symbol size may vary but the shape should remain the same. A flowchart template may be purchased in order to draw neat flowcharts.

1 *Flowlines* with arrows indicating direction. The standard direction of flow is from top to bottom, left to right.

2 *A connector* may be used to represent an exit from or an entry to

another part of the flowchart. It can also be used as a flowline connector.

3   *A process box* represents any kind of process for which there is no specific symbol.

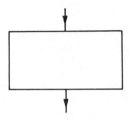

4   *Input/output*: this symbol represents an input/output function. Information is made available to the program, or input. Information created by the program is recorded, or output.

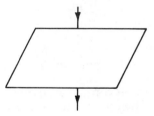

5   *Decision*, a diamond shape, is used to indicate a question. If the question is true then one exit will be taken, if it is untrue then another is taken. The true, untrue paths are indicated by a √ or x.

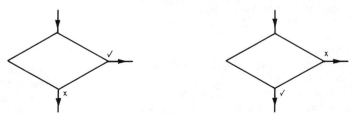

6   *Terminal*, a symbol used to start or stop the logic.

Flowcharts are written on plain paper. As they will often cover many pages, ensure that the pages are clearly numbered.

- The flowchart represents the sequence that the computer will execute, i.e. it obeys each instruction.
- The flowlines have arrows which direct you to the next instruction.
- The decision box has two output flowlines; the answer to the question asked in the decision box determines which flowline to follow.

The symbols in the flowchart should contain appropriate and descriptive text. The connectors should contain a reference, perhaps a letter, a letter group, or a number sequence. This reference can usefully be used later in the COBOL program.

The specification of the program must be read and fully understood before logic design commences. The specification must state what data will be input to the program, what processes the program must make on that data, and what results are to be output. Here is a specification of a program that you will code in chapter 4.

1   Identification
Program identifier. SALT.

2   Introduction
This program reads every record on a salary file and accumulates the salary on each record. The total of all the salaries is printed at the end of the program.

3   Processing tasks
(a) To read every record on the salary file.
(b) Accumulate the salary field.
(c) Print the final total.

4   Data
The salary file is held on a disc and has a name of DA01. The data is held in 7-character records, containing two fields: record type, a 1-character alphanumeric field, will contain 1, 2, A or B; salary, a 6-digit numeric field, may contain a value from 000000 to 999999.

5 Results
A printed total.

6 Processing
(a) The salary file must be opened and the salary total set to zero.
(b) A record should be read and a test made to see if the end of file has been reached.
(c) If end of file then the salary total will be printed, the salary file closed and the program stopped.
(d) If not end of file then the salary field on the record is added to the salary total and another record is read.

This is a simple specification but it gives you an idea of the way a program specification might be presented.

Fig. 2 shows the logic design for this program. The program logic starts with the appropriate 'sausage' shaped symbol and a connector, A. The next box is a process box containing two instructions: open the file and set salary total to zeros. The next symbol is a connector with the symbol B. Next there is a parallelogram for the input process: read salary file. A question is asked: is it the end of file? If this is the decision a control line goes to connector C; if this is not the decision the logic passes to the next box. The process box adds the salary on the record, just read, to the salary total. Control line to connector B.

Connector C passes to a process box which prints the final total and closes the salary file. The program stops as it started with a 'sausage' shape.

Having drawn the logic diagram it must be proved to work. This is called dry running. You must make up some simple data to test the logic diagram. Six data records each with different salary values are used.

Record type	Salary
1	001000
2	999999
3	123456
1	000000
A	723450
B	619800
End of file	

Now run this data through the logic, one data record at a time. When the end of file is read, control should pass to C and the total, 2467705, should be printed. Having proved the logic you may code the program.

Flowchart   Program SALT   Page 1 of 1

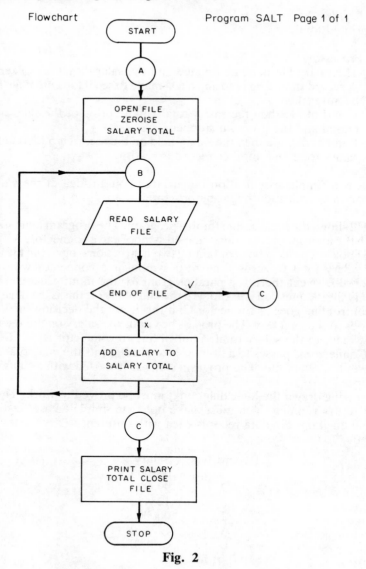

Fig. 2

There are examples of flowcharting throughout the book. The example program in chapter 14 (p. 142) shows you a more complex specification and the associated flowchart.

3

Introduction to COBOL

As computers developed and became more applicable to commercial work it was essential to make a computer easier to use for business use. The computer had been developed originally by scientists for scientists and it was necessary to bring computers into the business environment. The language of the computer had always been a numeric language or machine code – each make of computer had its own specific language. What was needed was a language that could be written by a business person. The language needed to be easy to write and understand and, ideally, available on any make of computer. COBOL was developed, under the auspices of the United States government, and was made available to all computer manufacturers. It was accepted by computer manufacturers and, in the early 1960s, an organisation was formed to standardise the COBOL language. The American National Standards Institute (ANSI) is the body that issued the first COBOL standard, and it is this body that provides new standards. These new standards are published at 4–6 year intervals.

COBOL is an English-based language, easy to write and sufficiently 'English-like' to be self-documentary. Like any language it has rules of grammar, or syntax rules. Unlike rules of grammar, which can be broken without making a sentence completely incomprehensible, syntax rules *must* be adhered to. The COBOL language is not understood by the computer, it is not a machine language. The written COBOL program is changed into machine language by a piece of software called a compiler. The compiler only understands correctly written COBOL and will indicate an error if any incorrect syntax is present in the program.

The program is written on special coding sheets. These sheets may differ slightly between manufacturers, but they are the same in essential details. The sheet consists of many lines, each line of coding being coded on a fresh line. Each line consists of 80 columns and a column can contain one character. The 80 columns on a coding sheet equate to a punched card which can contain 80 characters of information. The first 6 columns are called the *sequence number*. This can be used for numbering your program instructions, and is an optional facility.

Column 7 has a thick line on either side, and is called the *continuation area*. It can contain a *, or a -, or can be left blank. The use of these symbols will be explained later; the column is usually left blank. Columns 8–11 are called *Area A* and columns 12–72, *Area B*. Whenever a COBOL facility is described, the syntax rules will say that it must be present in either Area A or B. If Area A is stated, the coding must start in column 8; if Area B is stated then the coding may start anywhere from column 12–72. Columns 73–80, the *identification area*, must not contain COBOL coding; this area can be used to write comments or the identification of the program.

Throughout the book new COBOL facilities will be introduced, along with the formal syntax rules for that facility. First, we look at the way syntax rules are stated.

$$\underline{\text{WRITE}} \text{ record-name} \left[\begin{Bmatrix} \underline{\text{AFTER}} \\ \underline{\text{BEFORE}} \end{Bmatrix} \text{ADVANCING} \begin{Bmatrix} \text{integer} \\ \text{identifier} \end{Bmatrix} \text{LINES} \right]$$

All words printed in capitals are words reserved for the COBOL language. Words which are underlined are called *key words*: they are essential. Omission of these words will cause a syntax error. Words which are not underlined are optional or *noise words*; these words are not essential and omission will not cause a syntax error. They do, however, help the understanding of the coding and may be omitted at the programmer's discretion.

Words in lower case indicate that the programmer must supply the information. In the example we have record-name, data-name and integer, each one is to be supplied by the programmer. Integer is simply a whole number, e.g. 1 or 10. Record-name and data-name are names given to those pieces of information or data in order to identify them. How to use these will be explained later, but the rules for making up names in COBOL are as follows:

1   The name can be less than, or equal to, 30 characters in length.
2   The name can consist of the letters A–Z, the numbers 0–9 and a – (hyphen). The hyphen cannot start or end a name; the name must contain at least one non-numeric character.
3   The name may not be a COBOL reserved word. (See Appendix 1

for a full list.) E.g. COUNT is a reserved word, but you may use the name A-COUNT or, COUNT-1, or COUNTY.

4   The name must be unique within the COBOL program.

When choosing a name to identify a piece of data you should choose a meaningful name; remember COBOL should be self-documentary. Both FRED and AB–12 are valid data-names but their meaning is not clear. SALARY-TOTAL, STATION-CODE and RECORD-TYPE are both meaningful and valid COBOL names.

Braces { } indicate that you have a choice. One of the options must be taken.

Square brackets [ ] indicate that the enclosed coding is optional. Omission of the coding in the brackets can completely change the meaning of the statement.

Ellipses (. . .) indicate that the preceding code may be repeated once or many times.

Punctuation is part of the COBOL language just as it is part of the English language. Commas (,) and semi-colons (;) may be used, but are optional. The full stop (.) is not optional. It appears at the end of each sentence; a sentence can consist of one or more COBOL statements. Use a full stop at the end of each statement unless told otherwise. Omission of a full stop can cause syntax errors.

This is a correct COBOL statement obeying the syntax rules:

WRITE A-RECORD BEFORE ADVANCING 3 LINES.

A-RECORD is a programmer-supplied name. BEFORE has been chosen, ADVANCING and LINES are optional words and 3 is an integer value. We can say exactly the same without the noise words:

WRITE A-RECORD BEFORE 3.

To use this statement without the optional facilities held in [ ]:

WRITE A-RECORD.

This has a different meaning to the previous two examples but is syntactically correct.

Note that all the coding is written in capitals, and there is a full stop at the end of the statement.

A COBOL program is divided into four divisions. These divisions must be written in the correct sequence and each division must be introduced by a *division header*.

The *identification division* does what it says: it identifies the program. Like a book, it contains the program title or name, the author's name, the date written and explanatory remarks about the program.

The *environment division* describes the environment in which the program will be run. It connects the COBOL program with the computer functions external to the program. As it defines the environment the content of this division varies between versions of COBOL on different computers; however its function does not vary.

The *data division* sets out the data needed for the program: it describes and names the area of store allocated for each piece of data. It defines input and output data as well as working totals, constants and headings.

The *procedure division* is the division where the instructions are written. These instructions process the data and produce the necessary program results. This coding must follow exactly the logic of the flowchart.

Your finished COBOL coding is called a *source program*, the beginning. The source program is read by the *compiler*. The compiler does two things. Firstly, it checks each COBOL statement for syntax errors and prints both the source program and the errors found. Secondly, it breaks the COBOL coding down into machine-understood code. This machine code is called the *object program* and can be understood by the computer. To use or *run* your program, the object program is put into the computer. This process is called *loading*. Once the machine code is loaded into the computer's store, then the computer can obey the instructions. We say that the computer *executes* these instructions. The instructions are executed in exactly the same logical order that you have written them in your COBOL program. If the results produced by the computer are wrong, then your COBOL program must be wrong. It is rarely the computer that makes a mistake!

To summarise:

 – The COBOL language has syntax rules which must be obeyed.
 – Each COBOL facility must be written in the correct Area of the coding sheet: Area A and Area B are the most used parts of the coding sheet. Each COBOL sentence must be completed by a full stop. A sentence can consist of one or more COBOL statements.
 – The COBOL compiler reads and checks the program for syntax errors.
 – When writing your COBOL program you should write clearly in capitals.
 – The data preparation department must be able to read your code; bad writing can lead to data preparation errors.

It is important to differentiate between certain characters. I will use the following rules throughout the book. You should check your local standard as ø can be used to represent zero or alphabetic 0.

Numbers	Letters
0	ø
1	I
5	$

Throughout the book △ will be used to denote a space. You do not need to use this symbol in your coding but you should leave a blank column instead.

4

Coding a Simple Program

We shall now write the COBOL coding for the program flowchart which was produced in chapter 2. The first two COBOL divisions are the *identification* and *environment divisions*, they are relatively short and will not be covered again in this book. The *data* and *procedure divisions* will be very small as the program is simple.

Identification division

The purpose of this division is to name the program and to give other optional information about who wrote it, when it was written, etc. Here is the structure of the division; the entries are coded in Area A.

```
IDENTIFICATION DIVISION.
PROGRAM-ID. program-identifier.
AUTHOR. sentence(s) of comment.
INSTALLATION. sentence(s) of comment.
DATE-WRITTEN. sentence(s) of comment.
DATE-COMPILED. sentence(s) of comment.
SECURITY. sentence(s) of comment.
```

The PROGRAM-ID is supplied by the program specification and is the only mandatory paragraph in the division. The other paragraphs can contain relevant comment. It is useful to write a short comment about what the program does. This can be done by inserting an * in column 7 and writing any suitable comment on that line. This facility can be used anywhere in your COBOL program. The program will now read:

```
IDENTIFICATION DIVISION.
PROGRAM-ID. SALT.
AUTHOR. MELINDA FISHER.
*        THIS PROGRAM ACCUMULATES SALARY DETAILS.
```

Make sure that your division and paragraph names start in Area A and that you have remembered the full stops.

Environment division

This is so called because it describes the environment that the program will be compiled and run in. It names the computer, the files to be used by the program, and links the program with the operating system if necessary.

The structure of the division is:

```
ENVIRONMENT DIVISION.
CONFIGURATION SECTION.
SOURCE-COMPUTER.
OBJECT-COMPUTER.
INPUT-OUTPUT SECTION.
FILE-CONTROL.
```

Because it describes the environment, this division varies for different computer manufacturers. This program will use an ICL–2972 computer, the entries are straightforward and easily followed in a reference manual.

Configuration section

This section describes the computer on which the program is to be compiled and run. The entries are mandatory and written in Area A, the computer name varies depending on the machine being used.

```
ENVIRONMENT DIVISION.
CONFIGURATION SECTION.
SOURCE-COMPUTER. ICL-2972.
OBJECT-COMPUTER. ICL-2972.
```

Input-output section

File-control
This is the section and paragraph name for the statements that declare which files the program needs for input and output.

The format is:

```
SELECT filename
       ASSIGN TO implementor-name
       [ORGANISATION IS SEQUENTIAL]
       [ACCESS MODE IS SEQUENTIAL].
```

There must be a SELECT statement for each file used in the program. It is written in Area B. The file-name is a COBOL data-name that you make up: it will be used throughout your program to reference the file. The salary file has been named SALARY–FILE. The implementor-name is defined by the computer manufacturer.

The program has one file only – an input file whose implementor name is MS DA01. MS means that it is a disc file, and DA01 is the external name of the file. This information is given in the program specification.

The MS is documentary and may be omitted: it describes the peripheral that the file will be held on. MS is used for a disc file; LP is used for a line printer file: MT is used for a magnetic tape file: and CR is used for a card reader file. Remember the implementor name entry varies between manufacturers.

Our input-output section will look like this:

```
INPUT-OUTPUT SECTION.
FILE-CONTROL.
    SELECT SALARY-FILE ASSIGN TO MSΔDA01.
```

Data division

This division describes all data areas necessary for the program to work. The first section is the FILE SECTION. This describes the files and the records to be input and output by the program.

File section

For each file SELECTed in the INPUT–OUTPUT Section there must be an FD entry. The FD statement is coded in Area A, the other entries in Area B.

```
FD file-name
    [RECORDING MODE is mode-name]
    [ BLOCK CONTAINS [integer-1 TO] integer-2 { RECORDS    } ]
                                              { CHARACTERS }
    [RECORD CONTAINS [integer-3 TO] integer-4 CHARACTERS]
    [ LABEL { STANDARD }  ]
            { OMITTED  }
    [ VALUE OF implementor-name { data-name-1 } ]
                                { literal-1   }
    [ DATA { RECORD IS   } data-name-2 [data-name-3] ]
           { RECORDS ARE }
```

Only the file-name is mandatory, the other entries are optional and will vary depending on the computer and operating system being used.

In our program we have one file. This is what we would write:

```
DATA DIVISION.
FILE SECTION.
FD SALARY-FILE.
```

The file-name matches that in the SELECT statement of the FILE-CONTROL paragraph.

The computer program can deal with one input record at a time, therefore we need only describe the record once. An area is allocated in the computer's store to hold a record, called the *record buffer*. Each field of a record is described as it is stated in the program specification. The fields can be described and accessed exactly as we need to use them in our program. (To be able to access each field it must be named with a data-name. See chapter 3.)

There are two fields on the input record. A valid data-name is made up for each and written in the correct order.

You may also want to access the complete record, i.e. both record type and salary together. To do this, give this record a name.

```
SALARY-RECORD
RECORD-TYPE
SALARY
```

These are valid data-names, but how does the compiler know that the record-type and salary are fields belonging to the salary record? For this *level numbers* are used. Level numbers can be from 01–49, and need not be consecutive.

```
01 SALARY-RECORD.
   03 RECORD-TYPE
   03 SALARY
```

Use alternate numbers to allow for future amendments and indent each number for readability. You must start level numbers at 01.

The 01 level is coded in Area A, the other levels in Area B, for readability.

We have now described a record, SALARY–RECORD, that consists of two fields: RECORD–TYPE and SALARY. The 01 level data-name 'owns' the 03 levels.

We have not yet described how big the record-type and the salary fields are. We do this with the *picture clause*. PIC is a valid abbreviation.

RECORD–TYPE is a single character which can contain A, B, 1 or 2. It must be described as one character long and with a class of alphanumeric. Alphanumeric characters can hold any character, A–Z, 0–9 and all the special characters.

```
03 RECORD-TYPE   PIC X.
```

We use X to describe alphanumeric fields and one X means one character position. Full stop completes the clause.

SALARY is a 6-digit numeric field and must be described with a class of numeric as it is to be used in arithmetic. Numeric characters can hold any numeric digit from 0–9.

```
03 SALARY   PIC 999999.
```

We use 9 to describe a field with class numeric, each 9 representing a character position. It can be written in a shorthand form showing the class and (in brackets) the number of characters in the field:

```
03 SALARY   PIC 9(6).
```

A 20-character alphanumeric field will look like this:

```
PIC X(20).
```

If the class of data is alphabetic then A is used. An alphabetic character can hold A–Z and space.

```
PIC A(20).
```

This describes a 20-character alphabetic field.

```
DATA DIVISION.
FILE SECTION.
FD SALARY-FILE.
01 SALARY-RECORD.
   03 RECORD-TYPE     PIC X.
   03 SALARY          PIC 9(6).
```

The FD entry is used to connect the record description with the SELECT statement. The record buffer is described with the name SALARY–RECORD which has two fields, one alphanumeric and one character long, and the other numeric and 6 digits long. These two fields are called *elementary fields* and have picture clauses. SALARY–RECORD is a group field and has elementary fields belonging to it; it has no picture clause and must have a full stop after the data-name. The group field has an implicit class of alphanumeric and is the same length as the total of its elementary fields: in this case, 7 characters long.

Let us look at group and elementary fields more carefully.

A record holds the name and address of a customer.

The record is a group field, it has a name and address belonging to it. The level number 01 must be used to start a record description.

```
01 DETAIL-RECORD.
```

A group field has no picture clause and a full-stop follows the data-name.

The name field is also a group field comprising initials 2 characters long and a surname of 15 characters long. The name belongs to the

DETAIL-RECORD and, therefore, has a higher level number. Remember the name is also a group field.

```
03 DETAIL-NAME.
```

Now we can describe the initials and the surname. They belong to DETAIL–NAME and must have a higher level number.

```
05 DETAIL-INITIALS        PIC XX.
05 DETAIL-SURNAME         PIC X(15).
```

We have now given DETAIL–NAME a size of 17 characters and because it is a group field, an implicit class of alphanumeric.

The two fields, initials and surname, are elementary fields. They have picture clauses. Elementary fields must not have subordinate fields.

The next field is the address which comprises: a house number of 4 characters, a street name of 20 characters and a town name of 20 characters.

The address is, therefore, a group field which belongs to DETAIL–RECORD and follows DETAIL–NAME in the record. It will have the same level number as the name, but it does not belong to the name.

```
03 DETAIL-ADDRESS.
```

The number, street and town belong to DETAIL–ADDRESS and have a higher level number.

```
05 DETAIL-NUMBER          PIC 9(4).
05 DETAIL-STREET          PIC X(20).
05 DETAIL-TOWN            PIC X(20).
```

We have now given DETAIL–ADDRESS a size of 44 characters and an implicit class of alphanumeric.

The complete record description would look like this:

```
01 DETAIL-RECORD.
   03 DETAIL-NAME.
      05 DETAIL-INITIALS        PIC XX.
      05 DETAIL-SURNAME         PIC X(15).
   03 DETAIL-ADDRESS.
      05 DETAIL-NUMBER          PIC 9(4).
      05 DETAIL-STREET          PIC X(20).
      05 DETAIL-TOWN            PIC X(20).
```

We have given DETAIL–RECORD a size of 61 characters and an implicit class of alphanumeric.

By using level numbers we can build complex data descriptions.

Remember to use descriptive data-names and to indent the level numbers. This will aid understanding of the data.

Working-storage section

The second section in the data division is the working-storage section. Data areas are described in the same way as in the file section with level numbers, data names and picture clauses, but this time data areas are programmer-defined. Working-storage sets up work areas for the program processes: totalling fields, flags, storage areas. In this program there is only one working-storage area, the salary total field.

```
WORKING-STORAGE SECTION.
01 SALARY-TOTAL              PIC 9(8).
```

Salary-total is an elementary field, it is not part of a record and has no sub-fields. Notice the picture is numeric, because it will be used in arithmetic, and is 8 digits in length. The program totals many 6-digit numbers, therefore we must allocate a large enough totalling area.

Procedure division

This is the division that codes instructions in COBOL. These instructions must follow the logic of the flowchart and the words which specify the actions are called COBOL verbs.

The first verb used is the OPEN verb. A file, like a book, must be opened before it can be read or written. When a file is opened the compiler must be informed whether the file is for input or output or both, so that the computer knows the *mode* in which the file is to be used. You must also state the name of the file.

The format is:

$$\underline{\text{OPEN}} \left\{ \begin{array}{l} \text{INPUT} \\ \text{OUTPUT} \\ \text{I--O} \end{array} \right\} \text{filename-1...}$$

Our program will look like this:

```
PROCEDURE DIVISION.
AA-START.
     OPEN INPUT SALARY-FILE.
```

A paragraph name is needed to start the procedure code (a paragraph name obeys the same rules as other COBOL names); it is written in Area A. AA-START describes connector A and indicates that the program starts here and open is the first instruction executed by the computer. All verbs are written in Area B. The program reads data, therefore it is an input file. Notice the file-name matches the FD and the SELECT file-name.

Move

Next you must make sure that the total field SALARY–TOTAL has zeros in it before totalling begins.

We use the MOVE statement for moving data into one or more areas of the data division. The format is:

```
MOVE identifier-1 TO identifier-2 ...
```

The content of identifier-1 is moved to identifier-2; at the end of the move both areas will contain the same. (Note that an identifier is a COBOL data-name.)

Identifier-1 and identifier-2 might not be the same size. When moving alphanumeric and alphabetic identifiers, PIC X and A, data is always moved left justified and truncation will take place on the right if the receiving field is smaller. If the receiving field is larger then spare character positions are space filled.

```
MOVE A-FIELD TO B-FIELD.
          A-FIELD                    B-FIELD

PIC X(3).    A B 1          PIC X(3).    A B 1
PIC X(4).    A B / 2        PIC X(3).    A B /
PIC X(3).    A B /          PIC X(4).    A B / Δ
```

When moving numeric data PIC 9, data is always moved right justified and truncation will take place on the left if the receiving field is smaller. If the receiving field is larger then spare digits are zero filled.

```
MOVE X-FIELD TO N-FIELD.
          X-FIELD                    N-FIELD
PIC 9(3).  1 2 3            PIC 9(3).  1 2 3
PIC 9(4).  1 2 3 4          PIC 9(3).  2 3 4
PIC 9(3).  1 2 3            PIC 9(4).  0 1 2 3
```

The move really aligns itself with the decimal point. The decimal point is implicitly to the right of an integer field.

```
PIC 9(4).  1 2 3 4 ↑
               implied  decimal  point
```

There are many occasions when you want to move a value to a field. In this program you will want to move zeros to the salary total. COBOL supplies *figurative-constants*, a COBOL term which describes commonly needed data values.

```
ZERO(S)        HIGH-VALUE(S)        QUOTE(S)
SPACE(S)       LOW-VALUE(S)
```

Zero, space and quotes are self-explanatory, LOW-VALUES is the smallest value possible in a character, HIGH-VALUES the highest value possible in a character, see Appendix 3.

```
      MOVE SPACES TO A-FIELD.
                                 BEFORE                    AFTER
    01 A-FIELD PIC X(6).         1 2 7 / A T         Δ Δ Δ Δ Δ Δ
```

The terms SPACE or SPACES can both be used.

Alphanumeric or alphabetic fields cannot be moved to numeric fields but numeric fields can be moved to alphanumeric fields. ZEROS is a numeric value, SPACE is alphanumeric.

In this program you will write:

```
    MOVE ZEROS TO SALARY-TOTAL.
```

The next instruction is to read the file. This instruction is in a new paragraph indicated by connector B on the flowchart. The verb to read is:

```
    READ filename AT END imperative statement(s).
```

The file-name matches the open input, the FD and the select statement. The file-name is always read – never the record name.

The AT END is a question, i.e. is it the end of the file?, represented by the diamond decision symbol on the flowchart. It tells the computer what to do if all the records have been read. An imperative statement is an unconditional action: in the READ verb the action or actions are to be executed if all the records in the file have been read, i.e. if the end of the file is detected. Note that AT END is not triggered by the last record but by the software label after the last record. This means there is no data left. The program will look like this:

```
    BB-READ.
          READ SALARY-FILE AT END GO TO CC-END.
```

The READ causes the first or next record on the file to be placed in the file's record buffer, in this program, SALARY–RECORD. Each record is moved into this buffer automatically by the READ, causing the preceding record to be lost to the program. Therefore all processing must be completed before another READ is issued.

Go To

This is a sequence control statement, which allows you to branch backwards or forwards around the program. The paragraph-name to which control is passed must be coded somewhere in the procedure division. If the file is at end then control will pass to CC-END. Paragraph CC-END has not yet been coded.

```
    GO TO paragraph name.
```

Add

If a record has been successfully read, it is now placed in the record buffer. If we want to add the salary to the salary total, the verb is ADD.

```
ADD identifier-1 TO identifier-2.
```

All identifiers in an ADD statement must be elementary and numeric. The content of identifier-1 is added to the content of identifier-2 leaving identifier-1 unchanged and identifier-2 with the accumulated result.

```
ADD X-FIELD TO N-FIELD.
        X-FIELD                           N-FIELD
                                       BEFORE      AFTER
  PIC 9(3) 1 0 0        PIC 9(3).      2 5 0       3 5 0
  PIC 9(3) 2 3 3        PIC 9(4). 1 2 0 0      1 4 3 3
  PIC 9(4) 1 2 5 0      PIC 9(3).      9 0 0       1 5 0
```

Note the addition is done and then truncation occurs when the result is placed in the receiving field N–FIELD. It is important to make the receiving field large enough to avoid this truncation. The program adds the salary amount held on the record, which has just been read, to a total in working-storage: SALARY–TOTAL.

```
ADD SALARY TO SALARY-TOTAL.
```

Now one record has been processed you need to get the next record from the input file. This is done by branching to the READ with another GO TO verb.

```
GO TO BB-READ.
```

BB–READ is the paragraph name of the code which begins READ. You must branch to the READ and not the OPEN: the file must only be opened once. This completes the processing loop for each record. Now code the end routine CC–END. This code is only executed once if the AT END has been reached. The salary total must be printed to be seen on the computer output.

The verb is DISPLAY and is used to output small amounts of information.

```
DISPLAY identifier.
```

Identifier is a field in the data division whose content will be displayed. In this program we want to see the content of SALARY–TOTAL.

```
CC-END.
     DISPLAY SALARY-TOTAL.
```

The processing task is now completed. Before instructing the computer to stop you must close any files that have been opened:

```
CLOSE file-name-1...
```

Note that when closing a file you do not state Input or Output.

```
CLOSE SALARY-FILE.
```

The final executed statement is:

```
STOP RUN.
```

This halts the program's execution. Remember:

1 Division, section, paragraph-names, FD and 01 levels start in Area A of the coding sheet.
2 All other data entries and procedure verbs are written in Area B.
3 All data division and procedure sentences must be completed with a full stop.
4 Data-names must be unique.
5 Paragraph-names should be descriptive and correspond with the flowchart connectors.

Here is the complete program:

```
IDENTIFICATION DIVISION.
PROGRAM-ID. SALT.
AUTHOR. MELINDA FISHER.
*       THIS PROGRAM ACCUMULATES SALARY DETAILS
ENVIRONMENT DIVISION.
CONFIGURATION SECTION.
SOURCE-COMPUTER. ICL-2972.
OBJECT-COMPUTER. ICL-2972.
INPUT-OUTPUT SECTION.
FILE-CONTROL.
     SELECT SALARY-FILE ASSIGN TO MS DA01.
DATA DIVISION.
FILE SECTION.
FD SALARY-FILE.
01 SALARY-RECORD.
     03 RECORD-TYPE              PIC X.
     03 SALARY                   PIC 9(6).
WORKING-STORAGE SECTION.
01 SALARY-TOTAL                  PIC 9(8).
PROCEDURE DIVISION.
AA-START.
     OPEN INPUT SALARY-FILE.
     MOVE ZEROS TO SALARY-TOTAL.
BB-READ.
     READ SALARY-FILE AT END GO TO CC-END.
     ADD SALARY TO SALARY-TOTAL.
     GO TO BB-READ.
CC-END.
     DISPLAY SALARY-TOTAL.
     CLOSE SALARY-FILE.
     STOP RUN.
```

It is simple, but complete. Check the completed code very carefully for
full stops, correctly written data-names and logic. The program is now
ready for dry running. Take the data that was used to prove the
flowchart and drive it through the coding. If the salary-total contains
02467705 at the end then the program is ready for data preparation.

Simple program quiz

1 What symbol is written in Column 7 to denote comment in your
  COBOL program?

2 Which entry in the identification division is mandatory?

3 In which section is the source-computer entry?

4 If the implementor name in the Select . . . Assign is LP LP03, what
  peripheral would it describe?

5 What is wrong with the following implementor name? MSMS01.

6 What is wrong with the following code?

```
FILE CONTROL.
    SELECTED FILE ASSIGN TO MT MTO4
```

7 What is wrong with the following code?

```
00 GROUP-FIELD.
    02 WS-PART       PIC 9X.
    02 WS-TYPE.
    02 WS-PART       PIC A.
        50 WS-NAME   PIC X(20.
```

8 What is the collective name given to:

```
SPACES, ZEROS, QUOTES?
```

9 What will be in B-FIELD after each of these MOVES have been
  executed?

```
        MOVE A-FIELD TO B-FIELD.
    A-FIELD          CONTENT        B-FIELD
    a) PIC 9(3).        714         PIC 9(4).
    b) PIC X(6).      ORANGE        PIC X(4).
```

10 What are the three modes of OPENing a file?

11 What do we call the area of the store allocated for the record?

12 What will be in B-FIELD after each of these ADDS have been
   executed?

```
ADD A-FIELD TO B-FIELD.
A-FIELD              CONTENT      B-FIELD          CONTENT
a) PIC 9(3).           157        PIC 9(3)           312
b) PIC 9(4)           1203        PIC 9(3)           744
```

13 What statement do you use to stop the program?

14 In which Area on the coding sheet do you write paragraph-name?

15 Which of the following data entries are group fields and which are
    elementary fields?

    a) 01 DATA-RECORD PIC X(10).
    b) 03 MONTH-TOTALS.
    c) 01 MASTER-RECORD.

5

Data Division

In chapter 4 some simple data entries were described, in the file and the working-storage sections.

Display data

In order to understand the way data areas are allocated to storage areas we need to look inside the computer's memory or store.

Store consists of millions of bits, a bit being the smallest element of store, and is capable of holding the value 0 or 1.

Different machines have different methods of grouping these bits to form bytes, characters and words of various lengths. The following describes one of the most common ways of organising the computer's store using a 32-bit word. Words can also be 8, 16 and 24 bits long.

Bits are grouped into groups of 8 which are called bytes and the bytes are grouped into groups of 4 which are called words – hence the 32-bit long word.

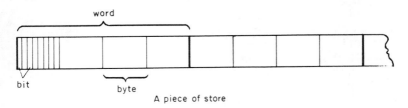

A piece of store

When you describe data in the data division, a piece of store is allocated and can be referenced by the data-name of that piece of store.

The data we described with PICTURE X, A and 9, where for each X, A or 9 stated in the picture clause a byte or character of store was set aside, is called DISPLAY data. The full syntax of a picture clause is:

```
level-number data-name data description usage clause
     01 TOTAL-MONEY         PIC 9(6)   [USAGE DISPLAY].
```

The USAGE DISPLAY clause is optional, and if omitted is assumed.
If you say:

```
01 MANS-NAME          PIC X(20).
```

twenty bytes of store will be allocated, each byte capable of holding an alphanumeric character.

How are these characters represented in the byte?

A byte is 8 bits in length and therefore has the ability to hold binary data from 00000000 to 11111111. In order to make this more easy to understand a notation called EBCDIC (Extended Binary Coded Decimal Interchange Code) is used. The byte is nominally divided into two parts called quartets. Each quartet can hold binary 0000 to 1111 or decimal 0 to 15, i.e. 16 different values. Both quartets together can hold a combination of 16×16 different patterns; this is base 16 and is called *hexadecimal*. Therefore one byte can represent 256 different characters. Rather than use complicated bit patterns, we can describe the value in each quartet. The leftmost quartet is called the zone quartet, and the rightmost the numeric quartet.

Here is a list of the possible values in a quartet, the binary, decimal and EBCDIC representations:

binary pattern	decimal value	EBCDIC notation
0000	= 0	0
0001	= 1	1
0010	= 2	2
0011	= 3	3
0100	= 4	4
0101	= 5	5
0110	= 6	6
0111	= 7	7
1000	= 8	8
1001	= 9	9
1010	= 10	A
1011	= 11	B
1100	= 12	C
1101	= 13	D
1110	= 14	E
1111	= 15	F

So a byte 4 D has the bit pattern 0100 1101.

The character that is represented by this EBCDIC notation along with the decimal value can be found in Appendix 3. This list is called the machine's *collating-sequence*. Each character has a different decimal value, and this value determines where the character lies in the collating-sequence. This sequence is used in sorting, and when comparing values.

ASCII

EBCDIC is one method of using bit patterns to represent characters. ASCII, American Standard Code for Information Interchange, is another commonly used collating-sequence. It is important for you to know which collating-sequence your computer implements because it will affect the sorting of data and the results of comparisons.

Compare the important characters in the two collating-sequences.

EBCDIC	*ASCII*
SPACE	SPACE
special characters	special characters
A–Z	0–9
special characters	special characters
0–9	A–Z

Special characters are for example: =) (› ‹ . ,

In EBCDIC, numbers are greater than letters, in ASCII the reverse is true. EBCDIC will be used throughout this book.

Signs and decimal points

When describing numeric or 9 type data you may want to allow for a positive or negative value. To do this you describe the sign in the picture clause.

```
01 TOTAL-MONEY      PIC S9(6).
```

TOTAL–MONEY can now hold from −999999 to +999999. The sign does *not* increase the size of store allocated to TOTAL–MONEY, it is held in the rightmost character. A 3-digit number with a negative value of 123 will hold the sign in the byte containing 3, the rightmost byte. This sign is held in the zone quartet of that byte. If you do not use the s then the field cannot hold a negative value, and positive values will be assumed.

You may also wish to describe where a decimal point is held in a numeric field:

```
01 TOTAL-MONEY      PIC 9(4)V99.
```

This describes 4 integral digits and 2 decimal digits. The v describes where the implied decimal point is, it does not take up any more store. You may mix signs and decimal points.

```
01  TOTAL-MONEY        PIC S9(4)V99.
```

An s or v may appear once in a picture clause. 18 is the maximum size for a numeric data field.

```
01  TOTAL-MONEY        PIC 9(18).
```

Binary data

The computer uses data in binary form when it does arithmetic and it improves efficiency if you describe any numeric data that is involved in arithmetic as binary data. You do this using the usage clause. As with other numeric data you describe the data with 9.

```
TOTAL-MONEY        PIC 9(6) [USAGE] { COMPUTATIONAL }.
                                    { COMP          }
```

This describes a field able to hold a maximum value of 999999 but the usage comp directs the computer to hold it in binary form and instead of allocating 6 characters of store it will allocate 20 bits, enough storage to hold 999999 in binary form. So when you describe a binary field you describe its maximum value, and the computer allocates enough store. As you can see it saves store and it also helps the computer's efficiency. Binary data cannot be used on punched cards or line printers but can be used in working storage or on magnetic tape or disc records.

You can have signs and decimal points in binary data.

```
TOTAL-MONEY        PIC S9(4)V99 COMP.
```

The store allocated will be 21 bits, the sign occupies an extra bit which is held at the leftmost end of the data. Note that the word usage is a noise word and that comp is an acceptable abbreviation of computational.

To improve arithmetic efficiency even more, the data should be both binary and at the rightmost end of a word. To do this the usage clause is extended.

```
01  TOTAL-MONEY        PIC S9(4)V99 COMP SYNC RIGHT.
```

sync is an abbreviation of synchronised. Whenever you set up a totalling field you should use comp sync right.

If you are describing a record in the file section, and the data is 4 digits binary, then the picture is:

```
PIC 9(4) COMP.
```

This will occupy 14 bits and the store allocated will start on the next character. If the data is 4 digits binary synchronised then the picture is:

```
PIC 9(4) COMP SYNC RIGHT.
```

This will occupy a whole word or 32 bits. There is an important distinction between binary and binary synchronised.

Note that whenever the level number 01 is used, storage allocation starts at the beginning of the next word.

There is another usage to describe binary data.

```
                                    ⎧COMPUTATIONAL-5⎫
TOTAL-COUNT        PIC 1(7)  ⎨                ⎬.
                                    ⎩COMP-5          ⎭
```

The usage is COMP-5 and it is only used when the PICTURE 1 is used. For every 1 pictured 1 bit of store is allocated, in the example 7 bits of store will be allocated. The maximum value of TOTAL-COUNT is 127 which is the maximum decimal value that can be held in 7 bits of store.

If your program logic requires an indicator, switch or flag, that is a piece of data that has the value 1 or 0, then COMP-5 could be used.

```
01 SWITCHES.
   03 SWITCH-A       PIC 1 COMP-5.
   03 SWITCH-B       PIC 1 COMP-5.
   03 SWITCH-C       PIC 1 COMP-5.
```

You can use a sign but not a decimal point with a COMP-5 field.

```
01 TOTAL-COUNT        PIC S1(7) COMP-5.
```

8 bits of store will be allocated, one extra for the sign.

Packed-decimal data

If we look at numeric data held in hexadecimal form in Appendix 3 we can see that a 1 is represented by F1, an 8 by F8, etc. We call this form of numbers *external decimal*. The zone quartet is always an F. Therefore the computer can easily recognise numeric data without the zone quartet and this enables us to *pack* numeric data. The usage clause for this is COMPUTATIONAL-3 or COMP-3.

```
01 TOTAL-MONEY        PIC 9(7) COMP-3.
```

This describes a packed-decimal field able to hold a maximum value of 9999999. The storage allocated is 4 bytes.

```
BYTE        QUARTET

 ⌒           / \
 9  9        9  9      9  9      9  +
```

A sign is always held in the numeric quartet of the rightmost byte, the rest of the quartets hold a decimal digit each. You can see that a field of 7 bytes can be packed into 4 bytes. Packing and unpacking data is a simple process and COMP-3 is a useful usage for data fields that are to be totalled and printed.

Redefines

When data is described in a program it is described in a way that allows the program to do a task. If you are asked to describe a field 6 characters long named A-CODE, the program needs to use the first 5 characters as numeric and the last one as alphanumeric.

```
03 A-CODE.
   05 A-NUM    PIC 9(5).
   05 A-ALPH   PIC X.
```

Another program may read the same data but simply needs to print the code.

```
03 A-CODE    PIC X(6).
```

The same piece of data is pictured to suit a specific program.

Consider a field 6 characters long that is alphanumeric if the indicator field has a value of a 2, and numeric if the indicator field has a value of 3. We can define a field two different ways in the same program.

```
03 A-NUM        PIC 9(6).
03 A-ALPH REDEFINES A-NUM PIC X(6).
```

Picture the field once, then, using the same level number, picture it in another way.

Redefines cannot be used on an 01 level in the file section.

```
03 A-AREA.
   05 A-A     PIC 9(6).
   05 A-B     PIC 99.
03 B-AREA REDEFINES A-AREA PIC 9(6)V99.
```

A-AREA is not numeric and cannot be used in arithmetic; B-AREA describes the same store as A-AREA, and can be used in arithmetic.

Filler

When a program reads a file it does not necessarily reference all the fields on a record. It is unnecessary to give those unused data fields a name but an area of store must be allocated. Instead of a data-name the word FILLER may be used. FILLER may *not* be referenced by a verb, it may appear many times in a program and is, therefore, not unique.

```
01  A-REC.
     03  A-TYPE        PIC  X.
     03  FILLER        PIC  X(6).
     03  A-AREA        PIC  9(3).
```

The 6 characters of data described by FILLER cannot be referenced explicitly by the program. FILLER may be used at any level.

Value clause

The value clause can only be used in the working-storage section; if used in the file section a compilation error will occur. The value clause enables you to put an initial value in a storage area. This is done with an extension of the data description clause. The value clause has two rules: one for numeric data and one for non-numeric data.

Non-numeric value clause

This is used with PIC X and A fields.

```
01  MANS-NAME         PIC  X(20)  VALUE  "MR JOHN MARTIN SMITH".
```

The field is called MANS-NAME. It is 20 characters long and has an alphanumeric class. The value to be held in the 20 characters is MR JOHN MARTIN SMITH. A quote ('') is used to bound the value, the quote is not part of that value. We call this a non-numeric literal. The literal is 20 characters long exactly.

```
01  MANS-NAME         PIC  X(20)  VALUE  "JOHN SMITH".
```

JOHN SMITH is only 10 characters long and will occupy the first 10 characters of the 20 character area, the other 10 characters will be filled with spaces. We say that the value is left-justified and space filled. Remember the same rules applied to the MOVE verb, when using alphanumeric data.

```
01  MANS-NAME         PIC  X(20)  VALUE  "MR JAMES MARTIN SMITH".
```

is 21 characters long, too large for the 20 character field – this will cause a compilation error.

```
01  AA-TYPE           PIC  X  VALUE  "1".
```

You can hold any character in a PIC X field including numbers.

Numeric value clause

This is used with a PIC 9 field of any usage and has a maximum size of 18.

```
01 TOTAL-MONEY          PIC 9(6) VALUE 123456.
```

A field is called TOTAL–MONEY: it is 6 digits long and numeric display the value to be held in it is 123456. Note that you do not use quotes for a value in a numeric field – this is called a numeric literal.

```
01 TOTAL-MONEY          PIC 9(6) VALUE 123.
```

123 will occupy the right hand 3 characters of TOTAL–MONEY, the other 3 characters will be filled with zeros. We say that the value is right-justified and zero filled.

```
01 TOTAL-MONEY          PIC 9(6) VALUE 1234567.
```

The value is too long and will cause a compilation error.
    A PIC 9 field can only hold numeric data.

```
01 TOTAL-MONEY          PIC S9(6) VALUE −1234.
```

With a signed picture you can specify a minus or plus sign. If you omit the sign in the value a plus will be assumed.

```
01 TOTAL-MONEY          PIC 9(4)V99 VALUE 123.45.
```

The decimal point in the value will align with the implied decimal point in the picture giving .45 in the decimal positions and 0123 in the integer positions.

```
01 TOTAL-MONEY          PIC 9(4)V99 VALUE 1234.5.
```

will give ·50 in the decimal position and 1234 in the integer position.
    You can use signs and decimal points together.

```
01 TOTAL-MONEY          PIC S9(4)V99   VALUE −1234.56.
```

The usage clause does not affect the way you write the value, but does affect the way the value is held in store.

```
01 TOTAL-MONEY          PIC 9(6) COMP SYNC RIGHT
                                 VALUE 123456.
```

will place the binary value for 123456 in store.

```
03 SWITCH-A             PIC 1 COMP-5 VALUE 0.
```

will place binary zero in the bit called SWITCH-A.

```
01 TOTAL-MONEY          PIC 9(7) COMP-3
                                 VALUE 123456.
```

will place packed decimal 123456 in the store area called TOTAL–MONEY.
    The value clause allows you to place an initial value in store, which can be overwritten later in the program.

Notice that the COBOL statement can be spread over more than one line. Do not split a word across a line.

Data division exercises

1 What is wrong with the following?

(a)	01 WS-A	PIC XXVXXX.
(b)	01 WS-B	PIC X(6) COMP SYNC RIGHT.
(c)	01 WS-C	PIC SA(5).
(d)	01 COUNT	PIC 9(6).
(e)	01 WS-D	PIC 1(3).
(f)	01 WS-E	PIC 9(4) COMP-9.
(g)	01 WS-F	PIC 9(6)V99 COMP SYNC RIGHT
(h)	01 WS-G	PIC X(6) VALUE JUMPER.
(i)	01 WS-H	PIC 999 VALUE -123.
(j)	01 WS-I	PIC 999 VALUE 1234.
(k)	01 WS-J	PIC 99V99 VALUE 12V34.
(l)	01 WS-K	PIC XXX.
	03 WS-L	PIC XX.

2 Write the data division entry for the following:

   (a) A 7-digit numeric display field named WS-NUM with level 07.
   (b) A numeric display field with four integral digits and two decimal digits named WS-DEC with level 03.
   (c) An alphanumeric field 20 characters long named WS-NAME with level 01.
   (d) A 3-bit field with a sign named WS-BIT with level 05.
   (e) A binary synchronised field capable of holding a maximum size of 9999 named WS-BIN level 01.
   (f) A packed decimal field of 5 digits with a sign, named WS-PACK level 03.

3 Write the correct value clauses for the following:

   (a) REPORT△△△ in PIC X(10).
   (b) 123 in PIC 9(5) COMP-3.
   (c) 23.50 in PIC 9(3)V99.
   (d) △△△△ DAY in PIC X(10).
   (e) zeros in PIC 9(6) COMP SYNC RIGHT.
   (f) ******* in PIC X(7).
   (g) 3 in PIC 1(2) COMP-5.

4 Write the following record description entry.

DA–TYPE	1 character alphanumeric.
DA–AREA	5 character alphabetic.
DA–CODE	4 characters numeric display.
.DA–AMOUNT	6 numeric display characters with a sign having 2 decimal digits.
DA–COST	6 numeric binary synchronised.

Note area and code will be accessed together as DA–GROUP and separately.

5 Write the following record description.

DA–TYPE	1 character alphanumeric
DA–ACCOUNT	3 character alphanumeric
DA–AREA	5 character alphabetic
DA–CODE	4 characters numeric display
DA–AMOUNT	7 packed decimal digits

Note area and code will be accessed together as DA–GROUP and DA–CODE will be accessed separately. DA–ACCOUNT is not referenced.

6 A field named A-FIELD is used as an 8-digit numeric display field and also an 8-digit alphanumeric field. Write the data description.

7 What will be the binary pattern in a byte if the byte contains the following EBCDIC values?

(a) 40   (c) C2
(b) F6   (d) 5B

8 What is the EBCDIC value for the following bit patterns?

(a) 0001 0000   (c) 1010 1101
(b) 1110 0111   (d) 1000 0011

9 Using Appendix 3, what characters are represented by the following EBCDIC values?

(a) 40   (d) 4B
(b) C3   (e) F2
(c) 60

6

Data Manipulation and Arithmetic

We have seen how data is described and how initial values can be assigned to those areas. There is another way of putting values into data areas, using data manipulating verbs. The first and most common is the MOVE verb (see chapter 4). Remember, verbs are written in Area B and are part of the procedure division. The MOVE verb always obeys the rules described in chapter 4. The data being moved and the receiving data area may be of any usage; the MOVE verb will automatically convert the data to be compatible with the receiving field usage.

```
MOVE   { literal-1    }  TO identifier-2 [identifier-3] ...
       { identifier-1 }
  .
01 TOTAL-FIELD         PIC S9(6) COMP SYNC RIGHT VALUE 1789.
01 WORK-FIELD          PIC 9(6).
      MOVE TOTAL-FIELD TO WORK-FIELD.
```

The binary field will automatically be converted to usage display and the result in WORK-FIELD will be 001789.

Assigning a value to a field does not ensure that value will always be there, it can be overwritten by a MOVE statement.

```
MOVE ZEROS TO TOTAL-FIELD.
```

TOTAL-FIELD did contain 001789 but will now contain binary zeros.

The rules concerning numeric moves become clearer with the use of V in a picture.

```
      .
      .
01 DECI-FIELD          PIC 9(4)V99 VALUE 1237.95.
01 INT-FIELD           PIC 9(4).
      .
      MOVE DECI-FIELD TO INT-FIELD.
```

The decimal point is aligned during the move resulting in the loss of the decimal positions, the result in INT–FIELD being 1237.

The sign is also important for a move statement.

```
01 SIGN-FIELD          PIC S9(4)V99 VALUE -172.33.
01 UNSIGN-FIELD        PIC 9(4)V99.

    MOVE SIGN-FIELD TO UNSIGN-FIELD.
```

The result will be 0172.33, the assumption being positive for an unsigned picture. The receiving field must be signed in order to preserve the sign of the sending field.

The MOVE statement treats group fields as an alphanumeric item.

```
    MOVE SPACES TO GROUP-FIELD.
01 GROUP-FIELD.
    03 GRP-1          PIC 9(4).
    03 GRP-2          PIC X(10).
    03 GRP-3          PIC 9(6)V99.
```

GROUP–FIELD is 22 characters long and each character will now contain a space character, despite GRP–1 and GRP–3 being numeric items.

When giving values to data fields in working-storage literals were introduced. Literals can also be used in the MOVE statement.

```
01 NUM-FIELD           PIC S9(4)V99.
    MOVE 123 TO NUM-FIELD.
    MOVE 123.45 TO NUM-FIELD.
    MOVE -1234.67 TO NUM-FIELD.
```

Remember you do not use quotes with numeric literals. The numeric literal must not contain spaces.

```
01 ALPH-FIELD          PIC X(6).
    MOVE "DONKEY" TO ALPH-FIELD.
    MOVE "B" TO ALPH-FIELD.
    MOVE "1273-A" TO ALPH-FIELD.
```

You can enclose any printable character from the collating-sequence in the quotes as this is a non-numeric literal.

To summarise, the MOVE is a commonly used and powerful verb. You can move any usage of data. You can use data-names, figurative-constants and literals as sending fields.

The rules of numeric moves are:

```
- aligned on the decimal point
- right-justified
- zero filled.
```

The rules of non-numeric moves are:

```
- left-justified
- space filled.
```

Initialise

There is another useful verb for placing values in data areas:

```
INITIALISE identifier-1 [identifier-2]...
```

As the name implies you will find this useful for setting fields to an initial value. It is of most use with a group field as the identifier.

```
01 GROUP-FIELD.
      03 A-FIELD      PIC X(6).
      03 B-FIELD      PIC A(10).
      03 C-FIELD      PIC 9(6).
      03 D-FIELD      PIC 9(6) COMP-3.
      03 E-FIELD      PIC 9(8) COMP SYNC RIGHT.
      03 FILLER       PIC X(7).
      03 F-FIELD      PIC X(5) VALUE "TOTAL".
       .
       .
      INITIALISE GROUP-FIELD.
```

Each field is given a value according to its class and usage.
PIC X and A fields are space filled.
PIC 9 fields are zero filled.

– C–FIELD will contain display zeros.
– D–FIELD will contain packed decimal zeros.
– E–FIELD will contain binary zeros.

A FILLER field will not be initialised. Note that F–FIELD will no longer hold the value TOTAL but will contain spaces.

Arithmetic verbs

Add
In chapter 4 a simple ADD statement was given.

$$\underline{ADD} \begin{Bmatrix} \text{literal-1} \\ \text{identifier-1} \end{Bmatrix} \begin{Bmatrix} \text{literal-2} \\ \text{identifier-2} \end{Bmatrix} \dots \underline{TO} \text{ identifier-3}$$
$$[\underline{ROUNDED}].$$

All literals and identifiers must be numeric, they may be of any usage.

```
ADD X-FIELD Y-FIELD TO N-FIELD.
```

X-FIELD	Y-FIELD	N-FIELD	
PIC 9(4)V99.	PIC 9(4)V99.	PIC 9(4)V9.	
		BEFORE	AFTER
0 1 2 7 5 3	4 0 2 1 1 2	0 0 3 0 5	4 1 7 9 1

Notice the truncation of the rightmost decimal position.

```
ADD X-FIELD Y-FIELD TO N-FIELD ROUNDED.
```

This statement would give a result in N–FIELD of 4179.2. The sum total of X–FIELD and Y–FIELD is 4179.15; there is no room for the 5 in N–FIELD. If that excess digit is 5 or larger then the next digit is rounded up. This form of the ADD overwrites the original content of N–FIELD. If the field content is to be unchanged the following format can be used:

$$\underline{ADD} \left\{ \begin{array}{l} \text{literal-1} \\ \text{identifier-1} \end{array} \right\} \left[\begin{array}{l} \text{literal-2} \\ \text{identifier-2} \end{array} \right] \dots \underline{GIVING} \text{ identifier-3}$$
$$[\underline{ROUNDED}] \qquad [\text{identifier-n } [\underline{ROUNDED}]] \dots$$

```
ADD X-FIELD N-FIELD GIVING Z-FIELD.

X-FIELD            N-FIELD            Z-FIELD
PIC 9(4). 7 1 4 0  PIC 9(3). 2 1 3    PIC 9(4). 7 3 5 3
PIC 99V9. 5 7 2    PIC 99V9. 3 0 4    PIC 999V9. 0 8 7 6
```

Z–FIELD may be ROUNDED – the effect is the same as described in the previous example. Note that the TO is not used when the GIVING option is present. The rest of the arithmetic verbs follow the same basic form.

Subtract

$$\underline{SUBTRACT} \left\{ \begin{array}{l} \text{literal-1} \\ \text{identifier-1} \end{array} \right\} \left[\begin{array}{l} \text{literal-2} \\ \text{identifier-2} \end{array} \right] \dots$$
$$\underline{FROM} \text{ identifier-m} \qquad [\underline{ROUNDED}]. [\text{identifier-n } [\underline{ROUNDED}]] \dots$$

or

$$\underline{SUBTRACT} \left\{ \begin{array}{l} \text{literal-1} \\ \text{identifier-1} \end{array} \right\} \left[\begin{array}{l} \text{literal-2} \\ \text{identifier-2} \end{array} \right] \dots \underline{FROM} \left\{ \begin{array}{l} \text{literal-m} \\ \text{identifier-m} \end{array} \right\}$$
$$\underline{GIVING} \text{ identifier-n } [\underline{ROUNDED}] [\text{identifier-0 } [\underline{ROUNDED}]] \dots$$

```
    SUBTRACT X-FIELD FROM Y-FIELD.
```

The content of X–FIELD will be taken from the content of Y–FIELD leaving the result in Y–FIELD.

```
X-FIELD            Y-FIELD
PIC 9(4).          PIC 9(6).
                   BEFORE          AFTER
7 3 2 4            0 9 8 1 3 4      0 9 0 8 1 0
```

It is good practice to describe the receiving field of a SUBTRACT with a sign in case the result is negative.

```
X-FIELD            Y-FIELD
PIC 9(6).          PIC S9(6).
                   BEFORE          AFTER
1 2 4 7 1 6        1 1 2 7 4 8      - 0 1 1 9 6 8
```

If Y–FIELD had not been signed the result would have been 011968.

The GIVING option can be used with the SUBTRACT verb.

```
SUBJECT X-FIELD FROM Y-FIELD GIVING Z-FIELD.
```

X–FIELD and Y–FIELD will remain the same and the result placed in Z–FIELD.

X-FIELD	Y-FIELD	Z-FIELD
PIC 9(6).	PIC 9(6).	PIC S9(6).
0 0 1 9 4 3	0 9 2 4 6 6	0 9 0 5 2 3

The ROUNDED option may also be used, the effect is the same as with the ADD statement.

Multiply

$$\text{\underline{MULTIPLY}} \begin{Bmatrix} \text{literal-1} \\ \text{identifier-1} \end{Bmatrix} \text{\underline{BY}} \text{ identifier-2 [\underline{ROUNDED}].}$$

or

$$\text{\underline{MULTIPLY}} \begin{Bmatrix} \text{literal-1} \\ \text{identifier-1} \end{Bmatrix} \text{\underline{BY}} \begin{Bmatrix} \text{literal-2} \\ \text{identifier-2} \end{Bmatrix}$$
$$\text{\underline{GIVING}} \quad \text{identifier-3} \quad \text{[[identifier-4]} \quad \text{[\underline{ROUNDED}]].}$$

```
MULTIPLY X-FIELD BY Y-FIELD.
```

The content of X–FIELD will be multiplied by the content of Y–FIELD, the result placed in Y–FIELD overwriting the original content.

X-FIELD	Y-FIELD		
PIC 9(4)V999.	PIC 9(5)V99.		
		BEFORE	AFTER
0 4 2 8 3 1 5		0 0 1 3 4 6 9	5 7 6 8 9 7 4

If the ROUNDED option had been used:

```
MULTIPLY X-FIELD BY Y-FIELD ROUNDED.
```

The result in Y–FIELD would be 57689747; the excess digit, 7, would cause the 4 to be rounded, leaving Y–FIELD containing 5768975.

The GIVING option may be used in order to preserve values in fields.

```
MULTIPLY X-FIELD BY Y-FIELD
         GIVING Z-FIELD ROUNDED N-FIELD.
```

X-FIELD	Y-FIELD
PIC 9(4)V99.	PIC 9(4)V99.
2 1 7 0 3 5	0 1 7 4 9 5

Z-FIELD		N-FIELD	
PIC 9(6).		PIC 9(6)V99.	
BEFORE	AFTER	BEFORE	AFTER
0 0 0 0 0 0	3 7 9 7 0 3	4 1 2 3 4 4	3 7 9 7 0 2 7 3

This example shows two receiving fields: z–FIELD rounded and N–FIELD not rounded. It is important to picture the receiving fields correctly to achieve the correct result. Notice that the initial content of the receiving fields z–FIELD and N–FIELD do not affect the result.

Divide

```
DIVIDE {literal-1  } INTO identifier-2 [[identifier-3]
       {identifier-1}
                            [ROUNDED]].
```

or

```
DIVIDE {literal-1  } INTO {literal-2  }
       {identifier-1}      {identifier-2}
    GIVING identifier-3 [[identifier-4] [ROUNDED]].
DIVIDE X-FIELD INTO Y-FIELD.
```

The content of Y–FIELD is divided by the content of X–FIELD, the result is placed in Y–FIELD overwriting the original content. The ROUNDED option may be used. The divisor, X–FIELD, must not contain zero, this will cause the program to stop with an error message.

```
DIVIDE X-FIELD INTO Y-FIELD GIVING
       Z-FIELD N-FIELD.
```

This is the same as the previous example but this time the result will be placed in z–FIELD and N–FIELD.

The divide verb follows the same pattern as the other arithmetic verbs except that you often require a remainder from a divide.

```
DIVIDE {literal-1  } INTO {literal-2  }
       {identifier-1}      {identifier-2}
    GIVING identifier-3
    REMAINDER identifier-4.
DIVIDE 365 INTO Y-FIELD
       GIVING Z-FIELD REMAINDER N-FIELD.
```

Y-FIELD	Z-FIELD		N-FIELD	
PIC 9(6).	PIC 9(4).		PIC 9(3).	
	BEFORE	AFTER	BEFORE	AFTER
7 5 7 9 8 7	1 2 4 1	2 0 7 6	0 0 1	2 4 7

The remainder of the division is placed in N–FIELD overwriting the original content.

Note that the numeric literal 365 has been used. Numeric literals may be used, but not as receiving fields.

Compute

```
COMPUTE identifier-1 [[identifier-2] [ROUNDED]]
```

$\left\{\begin{array}{l}\text{FROM} \\ = \\ \text{EQUALS}\end{array}\right\}$ arithmetic-expression.

The compute statement has a different format from the other arithmetic verbs. The result is placed in the first identifier or operand and not the last. More than one result field may be specified and the result field can be ROUNDED. The FROM, =, and EQUALS are synonymous; the = is the most commonly used.

The arithmetic expression is any valid equation, the operands are numeric identifiers or literals including figurative constant zero and the operators are as follows:

+ plus   − minus
/ divide by   * multiply by
** to the power of (exponentiation)

A simple example:

```
COMPUTE X-FIELD = N-FIELD — Z-FIELD.
```

This is the same as:

```
SUBTRACT Z-FIELD FROM N-FIELD GIVING X-FIELD.
```

A more complex example:

```
COMPUTE X-FIELD = N-FIELD / 43 * Z-FIELD + Y-FIELD * 205.
```

There must be a space either side of an operator and the equal sign.
    When the expression contains a mixture of operators the expression is evaluated in a fixed order.

1   ** exponentiation
2   */ multiply and divide
3   +− plus and minus.

The priority within this order is leftmost first. Therefore the expression will be evaluated thus:

> Divide 43 into N–FIELD giving work area–1
> Multiply Z–FIELD by work area–1
> Multiply Y–FIELD by 205 giving work area–2
> Add work area–1 to work area–2 giving X–FIELD.

This describes the evaluation sequence not the correct use of intermediate work areas.

N-FIELD PIC 9(6)	Y-FIELD PIC 9(4)V99	Z-FIELD PIC 9(4)	X-FIELD PIC 9(8)V99
1 7 4 2 3 6	0 1 3 8 0 1	0 9 4 2	0 3 8 4 5 2 7 6 0 5

The order of evaluation may not give you the correct result.

```
N-FIELD                    =        X-FIELD
Z-FIELD * Y-FIELD
```

This expression could be coded:

```
COMPUTE X-FIELD = N-FIELD / Z-FIELD * Y-FIELD.
```

N-FIELD	Z-FIELD	Y-FIELD	X-FIELD
PIC 9(5).	PIC 9(3)	PIC 9(3)	PIC 9(6)
4 0 7 6 5	0 3 1	0 0 5	0 0 6 5 7 5

This is incorrect. By using brackets we can impose a different evaluation sequence. The brackets will be evaluated first.

```
COMPUTE X-FIELD = N-FIELD / (Z-FIELD * Y-FIELD).
```

The result in x-FIELD will now be 000263, which is correct.

Remember to leave spaces on either side of the operators.

Data manipulation and arithmetic exercises

1 What does BB-FIELD contain after the MOVE has been executed?

```
        MOVE AA-FIELD TO BB-FIELD.
(a)     03 AA-FIELD          PIC 9(5).    17613
           05 BB-FIELD       PIC 9(3).
(b)     03 AA-FIELD          PIC 9(4).    4987
              07 BB-FIELD    PIC 9(6).
(c)           07 AA-FIELD    PIC 99V99.   1250
        03 BB-FIELD          PIC 999V9.
(d)        05 AA-FIELD       PIC 9(4)V99. 127835
           05 BB-FIELD       PIC 9(6).
(e)           07 AA-FIELD    PIC X(3).    ABC
              09 BB-FIELD    PIC X(5)
(f)     03 AA-FIELD.
           05 AA             PIC 9(4).    1234
           05 BB             PIC X(5)     ABCDE
        03 BB-FIELD          PIC X(6).
```

2 Show contents of these data items after the statement has been executed.

		BEFORE	AFTER
(a)	ADD A-NUM TO B-NUM.	A-NUM = 13	A-NUM =
		B-NUM = 11	B-NUM =
(b)	ADD A-NUM 20 GIVING B-NUM.	A-NUM = 100	A-NUM =
		B-NUM = 200	B-NUM =
(c)	ADD A-NUM TO B-NUM.	A-NUM = 26	A-NUM =
		B-NUM = 13.5	B-NUM =

(d)	SUBTRACT A-NUM FROM B-NUM.	A-NUM = 60	A-NUM =
		B-NUM = 120	B-NUM =
(e)	SUBTRACT A-NUM FROM B-NUM	A-NUM = 12.5	A-NUM =
	GIVING C-NUM.	B-NUM = 27.7	B-NUM =
		C-NUM = 050	C-NUM =
(f)	MULTIPLY 10 BY A-NUM.	A-NUM = 032	A-NUM =
(g)	MULTIPLY A-NUM BY B-NUM.	A-NUM = 70	A-NUM =
		B-NUM = 10	B-NUM =
(h)	MULTIPLY A-NUM BY 7 GIVING	A-NUM = 1.35	A-NUM =
	B-NUM ROUNDED.	B-NUM = 100.5	B-NUM =
(i)	DIVIDE 5 INTO A-NUM.	A-NUM = 15	A-NUM =
(j)	DIVIDE 12 INTO A-NUM	A-NUM = 100	A-NUM =
	GIVING B-NUM REMAINDER C-NUM.	B-NUM = 24	B-NUM =
		C-NUM = 10	C-NUM =

3 A man's pay is calculated by multiplying the hourly-rate by hours worked deducting insurance and 30% tax, and adding a bonus.

man's pay	NET-PAY	PIC 9(6)V99.
hourly-rate	HOUR-RATE	PIC 99V99.
hours worked	HOURS	PIC 999V99.
insurance	INSURE	PIC 99V99.
bonus	BONUS	PIC 99V99.

Write the necessary COBOL to calculate NET-PAY.

4 Write COMPUTE statements for the following:

(a) $\dfrac{\text{A-NUM} + \text{C-NUM} - 70}{\text{B-NUM}} = \text{X-NUM}$

(b) $\dfrac{\text{A-NUM} \times 60}{\text{B-NUM}} = \text{X-NUM}$

7

Sequence Control

In chapter 4 the simplest sequence control statements, GO and STOP, were introduced.

Program logic is rarely that simple. During a program, decisions have to be made and actions done according to that decision. In flowcharting terms a diamond shape is used.

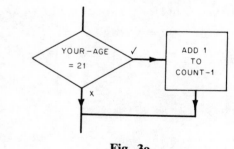

Fig. 3a

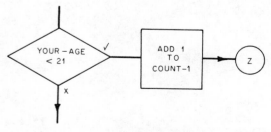

Fig. 3b

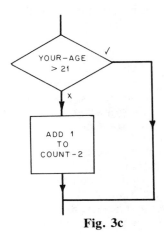

Fig. 3c

If

In COBOL the IF verb is used.

```
IF condition       {statement-1  }
                   {NEXT SENTENCE}
```

Let us first look at the condition which is the question or diamond in the flowchart. There are three types of condition:

relation
class
sign

Relation conditions are the most common.

Relation conditions

```
    {identifier-1         }           GREATER THAN   {identifier-2   }
IF  {literal-1            } IS [NOT]   >              {literal-2      }
    {arithmetic-expression}           LESS THAN      {arithmetic-    }
                                      <              {expression     }
                                      EQUAL TO
                                      =
```

For example:

```
IF MY-AGE IS GREATER 60
IF YOUR-AGE IS < MY-AGE
IF MY-AGE = YOUR-AGE
IF MY-AGE + 2 = YOUR-AGE + 10
IF MY-AGE NOT < YOUR-AGE
IF YOUR-AGE NOT = 21
IF A-CODE = "A"
```

These are all valid conditions or questions. Having asked the question an action is to be taken. (See Fig. 3a.)

```
IF YOUR-AGE = 21 ADD 1 TO COUNT-1.
  .
  .
```

The action ADD 1 to COUNT–1 will only be taken if the question is true, then control will automatically pass to the next COBOL sentence. If the question is not true control will pass to the next COBOL sentence. The full stop is very important here. More than one action can be taken. (See Fig. 3b.)

The statement used in the IF verb to describe the action to be taken is called an imperative statement.

The READ verb also used an imperative statement to be actioned when the end of file was read.

An imperative statement is a COBOL verb which is unconditional.

Later on in the book you will meet verbs like STRING and SEARCH that are not imperative verbs.

The verbs GO, ADD, etc, are imperative, but READ is not.

```
IF YOUR-AGE = 21 ADD 1 TO COUNT-1
                       GO TO Z-PARA.
  .
  .
  .
```

The full stop is at the end of the last statement to be actioned if the condition is true. If the condition is not true control will automatically pass to the next statement after the full stop. This is the next COBOL sentence.

There are two ways of coding Fig. 3c. No action is to be taken if the condition is true.

```
      IF YOUR-AGE = 21 GO TO X-PARA.
      ADD 1 TO COUNT-2.
X-PARA.
      .
      .
```

Or using the NOT option.

```
IF YOUR-AGE NOT = 21 ADD 1 TO COUNT-2.
  .
  .
  .
```

If YOUR–AGE is 21 then the ADD statement will be ignored and control passed to the statement after the full stop.

It is sometimes easier to code the negative condition by using NOT, but be careful as it may make the code less easy to understand.

You can compare data-areas of different sizes and usages. Data of different usage will be converted to a compatible form before comparison takes place. Data of different size will be expanded to be of equal size before comparison takes place. Expansion obeys the normal rules of right-justified zero filled for numeric data and left-justified space filled for non-numeric data.

To compare the value of different characters the collating-sequence is used, characters at the beginning of the sequence have a lower value than characters at the end of the sequence. (See Appendix 3.)

```
        IF A-FIELD > B-FIELD
           GO TO Z-PARA.
A-FIELD            B-FIELD        Will control pass to
                                     Z-PARA?
C A T △            C A T             NO
C A T              D Ø G             NO
1 2 3              1 2 A             YES
0 1 2 3            1 2 3             NO
9 9 9              Z Z Z             YES
```

Class conditions

```
IF identifier-1 IS [NOT]    ⎧NUMERIC      ⎫
                            ⎨ALPHABETIC   ⎬
                            ⎩ALPHABETIC-1 ⎭
```

For example:

```
IF MY-NAME IS ALPHABETIC
IF YOUR-TOWN IS ALPHABETIC-1
IF MY-NUMBER IS NUMERIC
IF YOUR-NUMBER IS NOT NUMERIC
```

This condition tests the contents of the identifier to see if it is all of one class, if any character does not belong to that class then the condition is not true.

- NUMERIC tests for characters 0–9 and may include a sign in the correct position.
- ALPHABETIC tests for characters A–Z and space.
- ALPHABETIC–1 tests for characters a–z, A–Z and space.

This is useful for validation of data.

You are permitted to use the class test on the following PICTURES indicated by √.

	[NOT] NUMERIC	[NOT] ALPHABETIC(—1)
PIC A	X	√
PIC X	√	√
PIC 9	√	X

For example:

```
IF THE-STREET NOT ALPHABETIC
   GO TO INVALID-PARA.
IF THE-NUMBER NUMERIC
   GO TO VALID-PARA.
```

Sign condition

```
IF identifier-1 IS [NOT]    {POSITIVE
                             NEGATIVE
                             ZERO    }
```

For example:

```
IF NUM-FIELD NOT POSITIVE
IF NUM-FIELD ZERO
IF NUM-FIELD NEGATIVE
```

This condition is only valid with a numeric signed field. A field containing ZEROS is neither POSITIVE nor NEGATIVE.

```
IF NUM-FIELD POSITIVE ADD 1 TO COUNT-1.
IF NUM-FIELD NEGATIVE ADD 1 TO COUNT-2.
                             GO TO NEG-PARA.
```

Else

Decision boxes often look like Fig. 4a, with a different action for the true and false paths.

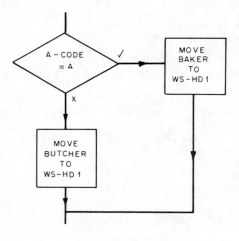

Fig. 4a

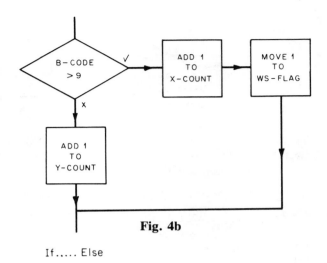

Fig. 4b

If..... Else

This is coded in COBOL with an

<u>IF</u> condition $\left\{\begin{array}{l}\text{statement-1}\\ \text{NEXT SENTENCE}\end{array}\right\}$ <u>ELSE</u> $\left\{\begin{array}{l}\text{statement-2}\\ \text{NEXT SENTENCE}\end{array}\right\}$

Fig. 4a can be coded:

```
IF  A-CODE = "A"
    MOVE "BAKER" TO WS-HD1
ELSE
    MOVE "BUTCHER" TO WS-HD1.
```

The full stop comes at the very end only. Notice the indentation, this helps make the statement more readable. You may split any COBOL statement over a number of lines. Do not split a word.

The statement may be one or more imperative COBOL verbs.

Fig. 4b can be coded:

```
IF  B-CODE > 9
    ADD 1 TO X-COUNT
    MOVE "1" TO WS—FLAG
ELSE
    ADD 1 TO Y-COUNT.
```

The ADD and MOVE could have been written on a single line. This format is neater.

A condition may consist of more than one decision, and is called a compound condition. The conditions are joined by AND and OR.

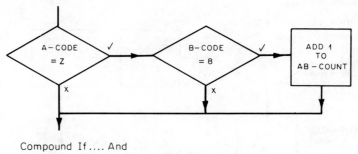

Compound If.... And

Fig. 5

And

Both A–CODE must = "Z" and B–CODE must = 8 for the action to be taken, it is coded this way.

```
IF A-CODE = "Z" AND
   B-CODE = 8
   ADD 1 TO AB-COUNT.
```

Or

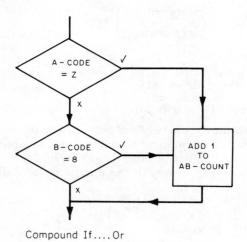

Compound If.... Or

Fig. 6

```
IF A-CODE = "Z" OR
   B-CODE = 8
   ADD 1 TO AB-COUNT.
```

The action is taken if A–CODE = z or B–CODE = 8.

Next sentence

The most common imperative statement used with the IF is GO TO. The IF is used to decide where control is passed to. Control can only be passed to a named procedure or paragraph name when using GO TO.

```
COMP-PARA.
      IF A-CODE = B-CODE
            GO TO MOVE-PARA
      ELSE
            ADD 1 TO UNEQUAL-COUNT.
MOVE-PARA.
      MOVE A-REC TO B-REC.
```

You can use NEXT SENTENCE instead of the GO TO.

```
COMP-PARA.
      IF A-CODE = B-CODE
         NEXT SENTENCE
      ELSE
         ADD 1 TO UNEQUAL-COUNT.
      MOVE A-REC TO B-REC.
```

NEXT SENTENCE passes control to the statement following the full stop. In this case we no longer need the MOVE-PARA paragraph name.

Complex conditions

Fig. 7 combines a class, relation and sign condition to make a compound condition and it has an ELSE path.

```
IF L-NAME ALPHABETIC AND
   W-TOTAL = 900 OR
   W-NUM NEGATIVE
      MOVE "XX" TO W-AREA
ELSE
      MOVE "ZZ" TO W-AREA
      ADD 1 TO A-COUNT.
```

Conditions linked by AND are evaluated before conditions linked by OR.

Go To depending

There is a useful verb which can be used when the content of a piece of data determines which paragraph is to be executed.

```
GO TO procedure-name-1 [procedure-name-2]...
    DEPENDING ON identifier.
```

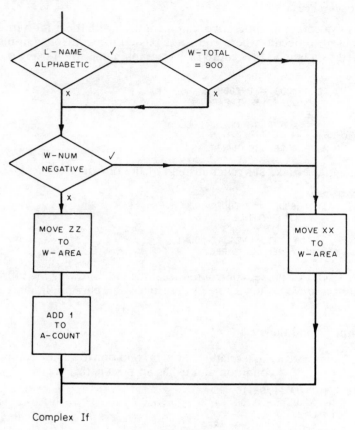

Complex If

Fig. 7

The identifier should be a numeric piece of data.

```
01 IN-REC.
   03 IN-CODE        PIC 9.
```

The value in IN-CODE will be 1, 2, 3 or 4.

```
PROCEDURE DIVISION.
  .
  .
  .
  .
    GO TO PARA-1 PARA-2 PARA-3 PARA-4
```

```
        DEPENDING ON IN-CODE.
  PARA-0.
     .
     .
     GO TO PARA-END.
     .
     .
  PARA-1.
     .
     .
     GO TO PARA-END.
  PARA-2.
     .
     .
     GO TO PARA-END.
  PARA-3.
     .
     .
     GO TO PARA-END.
  PARA-4.
     .
     .
     GO TO PARA-END.
  PARA-END.
     .
     .
     .
```

If the value in IN-CODE is 1 then control will pass to PARA-1, if it is 2 control will pass to PARA-2 and so on. There are four paragraphs named, this caters for values 1, 2, 3 and 4. If the value is 0 or greater than 4 then control will pass to PARA-0, the paragraph following the GO TO. This is only of use if IN-CODE contains values from 1 onwards. It would not work if the values were 2, 6, 7 and 9.

Condition-names

There is a format of the IF verb:

IF condition-name {statement-1 / NEXT SENTENCE} [ELSE {statement-2 / NEXT SENTENCE}]

Using a condition-name is another way of setting up a relationship test. For example, if a grade-code held on an input record is 6, 7 or 8 the record is for a junior who is entitled to 20 days' leave. If the grade-code is 3 or 5 the record is for a manager who is entitled to 24 days' leave. If the grade-code is 1 the record is for a senior manager who is entitled to 28 days' leave.

This can be coded using an IF relation test.

```
01 IN-REC.
   03 IN-GRADE        PIC 9.
```

To use the condition test the data field which is to be tested has extra entries immediately following it. These extra entries have a level number of 88. Each 88 level has a data-name which is called a condition-name; this is followed by a VALUE clause.

```
03 IN-GRADE        PIC 9.
88 JUNIOR          VALUE 6 THRU 8.
```

JUNIOR is a condition-name which is true if IN–GRADE has the value 6, 7 or 8.

```
88 MANAGER         VALUE 3 5.
88 SENIOR          VALUE 1.
```

MANAGER is a condition-name which is true if IN–GRADE has the value 3 or 5. SENIOR is a condition-name which is true if IN–GRADE has the value 1.

88 levels do not describe sub-fields in the way that levels 01–49 do. The value clause of an 88 level does not put a value into a field, but describes a value for the condition to be true. 88 levels may be used in the file and working-storage sections.

To use 88 levels in the procedure division:

```
PROCEDURE DIVISION.
      .
      .
      .
      IF JUNIOR MOVE 20 TO WS-LEAVE.
      IF MANAGER MOVE 24 TO WS-LEAVE.
      IF SENIOR MOVE 28 TO WS-LEAVE.
```

The compiler expands the condition-name into a relation test. It will expand IF JUNIOR . . . into

```
IF IN-GRADE > 5 AND
   IN-GRADE < 9 MOVE 20 TO WS-LEAVE.
```

This is a useful feature if the grade-codes are subject to frequent change. If grade-code 9 is added to the MANAGER range, all you change is the 88 level.

```
88 MANAGER VALUE 3 5 9.
```

88 levels can be used with non-numeric fields.

```
03 IN-CODE         PIC XX.
88 AREA-1          VALUE "AB".
88 AREA-2          VALUE "DE".
```

The value must obey the same rules as other value clauses.

Sections and perform

You have learned that the procedure division is made up of paragraphs and each is given a name. This name is written in Area A. The paragraph-name serves two purposes:

1 To enable control to be passed to that paragraph with a GO TO para-name;
2 To document the program by using a paragraph-name that describes the procedure logic in the paragraph.

Sections

You can divide your program into larger pieces than paragraphs. The section is named in the same way as a paragraph, but there is a space and the word SECTION following it. A section can contain many paragraphs.

```
MAIN-PROCESS SECTION.
```

As with paragraph-names the full stop must be present.

Sections serve the same two purposes described for paragraphs. You may say GO TO MAIN-PROCESS. Notice you do not say SECTION when using a GO TO. The SECTION name must be unique within the program and is written in Area A. A section name must be followed by a paragraph-name, e.g.

```
MAIN-PROCESS SECTION.
READ-PARA.
```

Perform

Having designed your flowchart you may notice that a certain sequence of logic is to be found in a number of places.

```
PARA-A.
      MOVE "A" TO FLAG.
      ADD 1 TO COUNT-A.
      MULTIPLY TOTAL-A BY TOTAL-B.
PARA-B.
      IF REC-TYPE = 7 GO TO PARA-Z.
      MOVE "A" TO FLAG.
      ADD 1 TO COUNT-A.
      MULTIPLY TOTAL-A BY TOTAL-B.
      .
      .
      .
      .
      MOVE "A" TO FLAG.
```

```
        ADD 1 TO COUNT-A.
        MULTIPLY TOTAL-A BY TOTAL-B.
        GO TO PARA-D.
 PARA-K.
```

You can see that the sequence

```
        MOVE "A" TO FLAG.
        ADD 1 TO COUNT-A.
        MULTIPLY TOTAL-A BY TOTAL-B.
```

appears in three places. Instead of writing it in full three times you can use the PERFORM verb.

PERFORM procedure-name-1 [{THRU / THROUGH} procedure-name-2].

The common piece of code must be exactly the same, the code must be written once and must be in a paragraph on its own. (See example.) PARA–A contains the common code. On the second and subsequent times the code is replaced by:

```
PERFORM PARA-A.
```

Therefore you write:

```
PARA-A.
        MOVE "A" TO FLAG.
        ADD 1 TO COUNT-A.
        MULTIPLY TOTAL-A BY TOTAL-B.
PARA-B.
        .
        IF REC-TYPE = 7 GO TO PARA-Z.
        PERFORM PARA-A.
   .
   .
        PERFORM PARA-A.
        GO TO PARA-D.
PARA-K.
   .
   .
```

The PERFORM passes control to PARA–A. When all the statements in PARA–A have been executed control is returned to the statement following the PERFORM. A GO TO PARA–A would *not* have been appropriate because control would not have returned to the correct statement.

```
PARA-H.
        READ A-FILE AT END GO TO PARA-L.
PARA-K.
        ADD 1 TO TOTAL.
        MOVE TOTAL TO PR-1.
        IF REC-1 = 4 GO TO PARA-L.
        ADD 1 TO A-COUNT.
```

```
PARA-L.
        MOVE A-COUNT TO PR-2.
        .
        .
PARA-M.
        .
        .
        PERFORM PARA-H THRU PARA-L.
```

The first statement in PARA–H through the last in PARA–L is executed by the PERFORM.

The procedure name in a PERFORM may be either a SECTION name or paragraph name.

You may write a PERFORM within a PERFORM but you must never use a GO TO which branches outside of the performed code.

```
PARA-H.
        READ A-FILE AT END GO TO PARA-L.
PARA-K.
        PERFORM PARA-Z.
        MOVE 1 TO PR-1.
PARA-L.
        MOVE A-COUNT TO PR-2.
        GO TO PARA-Z.
PARA-M.
        PERFORM PARA-H THRU PARA-L.
```

This example has a GO TO which is contained by the performed code. GO TO PARA–Z would have branched outside the performed code. This might cause a logic error but will not cause a syntax error.

Exit

In the previous example there is a READ statement with an AT END branch to PARA–L.

```
READ A-FILE AT END GO TO PARA-L.
```

PARA–L is the last named procedure-name in the PERFORM.

```
PERFORM PARA-H THRU PARA-L.
```

It is possible that having branched to PARA–L there is no code to be executed but that PARA–L is simply an EXIT or last paragraph.

EXIT is a verb, all on its own, in a paragraph used in this situation.

```
PARA-L.
     EXIT.
PARA-M.
```

When setting up a PERFORM that has many paragraphs it can be useful to have a final EXIT paragraph. This enables you to say PERFORM first-procedure THRU exit-procedure without knowing the actual code within those paragraphs.

```
CC-PROCESS.
      .
      .
      .
      .
CA-ADD.
      .
      .
      .
      .
CB-WRITE.
      .
      .
      .
      .
CC-EXIT.
      EXIT.
DD-MAIN.
      .
      .
      PERFORM CC-PROCESS THRU CC-EXIT.
```

It would, however, be easier to put these paragraphs in a section called CC SECTION and PERFORM the section.

```
CC SECTION.
CC-PROCESS.
   .
   .
   .
CA-ADD.
   .
   .
   .
CB-WRITE.
   .
   .
   .
   .
CC-EXIT.
      EXIT.
DD SECTION.
DD-MAIN.
   .
   .
   .
      PERFORM CC.
```

Sequence control exercises

1 Indicate whether control will pass to PARA–TRUE.

```
IF WS-CODE < A-CODE
        GO TO PARA-TRUE.
```

Both fields are alphanumeric.

```
    WS-CODE         A-CODE
(a) MESS            MESSY
(b) ABCD            1234
(c) ABC             ABCD
(d) ABC1            ABCZ
```

2 Write an IF statement for the following:
A field IN–ACCOUNT must contain numeric data and have a value greater than 110, if it does branch to PARA–VALID.

3 Write an IF statement for the following:
If a field IN–CODE has the value 3 branch to A–PARA if it does not add 1 to IN–COUNT and branch to the next statement.

4 Write an IF statement for the following:
If a field IN–NUM is negative add 10 to IN–TOTAL and move zero to IN–PART.

5 Write condition-name entries for the following:
IN–AGE is a 2-digit numeric display field, on an 03 level.
If its value is 0 to 17 then it is data for a minor, if its value is 18 it is data for a new adult, if its value is 65 it is data for a new pensioner. Three condition names will be required.

6 There are four mistakes in the following code. What are they?

```
MAIN-LOGIC SECTION.
    READ A-FILE AT END GO TO THE-END SECTION.
    .
    .
    .
OUTPUT.
    .
    .
    .
THE-END SECTION.
END PARA.
```

7 Given the following code:

```
SECT1 SECTION
PARA-A.
    .
    .
    .
```

```
PARA-B.
    .
    .
    .
PARA-D
    EXIT.
SECT2 SECTION.
    .
    .
    .
    .
```

which of the following statements are correct?

(a) PERFORM SECT1.
(b) PERFORM PARA-D THRU PARA-A.
(c) PERFORM SECT2 SECTION.

8 Code the following flowchart. (Do not make the coding too complicated.)

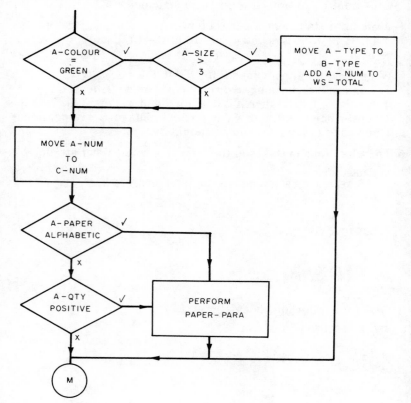

9 The following record is to be validated. Write the coding to validate this record. Each field must be checked in turn starting at the first field. If an error is found, control should be passed to paragraph ZZ–INVALID, if the complete record is valid then control should be passed to paragraph AA–VALID. Assume the record has been read for you. Start with the paragraph CC–VALIDATE.

```
01 IN-REC.
    03 IN-TYPE              PIC XX.
    03 IN-AMOUNT            PIC S9(6) COMP SYNC RIGHT.
    03 IN-QTY               PIC 99.
    03 IN-CODE              PIC X.
```

For a valid field:

TYPE must contain EF or XY.
AMOUNT must be numeric and positive.
QTY must be numeric and greater than 10.
CODE must be 1, 2, 3 or 4.

8

Sequential File Handling

This chapter describes in more detail how to handle sequential files. A sequential file is a file whose sequence is determined by the order in which the records were written when it was created. The name sequential does not mean that the file is in a key sequence, but describes a predecessor/successor relationship between consecutive records. Only the first and last records do not have this relationship. A sequential file can be sorted, i.e. a personnel number held in a record is sorted leaving the file in personnel number sequence: the personnel number is called the *key* field.

Sequential files are the most common and can be stored on any media, magnetic tape, disc, paper tape, cards, printer.

You have seen in chapter 4 a simple example of READing an input sequential file. This is an example of creating an output sequential disc file named DA02 from an input card file named CR01. Remember that the *environment division* establishes a link between your COBOL program and the machine's operating system.

```
ENVIRONMENT DIVISION.
FILE-CONTROL.
    SELECT CARD-IN ASSIGN CR CR01.
    SELECT AMEND-OUT ASSIGN MS DA01.
```

The files are described in the *data division*.

```
DATA DIVISION.
FILE SECTION.
FD CARD-IN.
01 CARD-REC.
    03 CARD-TYPE       PIC X.
    03 CARD-GROUP.
        05 CARD-AREA   PIC 9.
        05 CARD-CODE   PIC X(4).
```

```
        03 CARD-TOTAL-1    PIC 9(4).
        03 CARD-TOTAL-2    PIC 9(4).
*INPUT CARD RECORD - 3 VALID TYPES I, A, D.

  FD AMEND-OUT.
  01 AMEND-REC-1A.
        03 AMEND-TYPE-IA   PIC X.
        03 AMEND-GROUP-IA  PIC X(5).
        03 AMEND-NAME      PIC X(14).
        03 AMEND-TOTAL     PIC 9(6) COMP SYNC RIGHT.

*OUTPUT RECORD 1 - 2 VALID TYPES I, or A

  01 AMEND-REC-D.
        03 AMEND-TYPE-D    PIC X.
        03 AMEND-GROUP-D   PIC X(5).
        03 AMEND-DEL       PIC X(6).
*OUTPUT RECORD 2 - 1 VALID TYPE D.
```

For each valid input card record an output record is to be created, invalid records will be rejected. The type is to be checked for I, A or D. The area is to be checked for 1, 2, 3, 4. Depending on the area a name is created in the output record. Here are the names for each area code:

Area 1 – SOUTHERN
Area 2 – EASTERN
Area 3 – NORTHERN
Area 4 – WESTERN

The CODE field is moved to the output record without being checked. The two total fields are added together and placed in the output record.

Let us look at the output file. There are two 01 levels with different record descriptions. In this case one record describes a record which can be type I or A and the other describes a record with type D. This is called a multi-type record file. A file can have any number of record types: each format will be described with its own 01 level and each will be made up of different fields. The only field which must be common will be the record type which is usually at the start of the record and always in the same place, positionally, for each record. The compiler will set up an area of store large enough for the largest record. In this case AMEND–REC–IA is the largest; this area is called the *record buffer*. AMEND–REC–D will share this area with AMEND–REC–IA. Remember a program can only process one record at a time.

We will now write the *procedure division* for this program.

```
PROCEDURE DIVISION.
AA-START.
        OPEN INPUT CARD-IN.
        OPEN OUTPUT AMEND-OUT.
```

Record Buffer when it contains AMEND-REC-IA

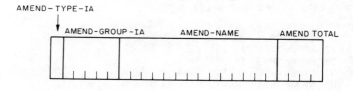

Record Buffer when it contains AMEND-REC-D

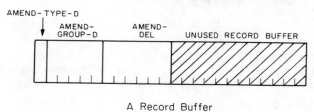

A Record Buffer

Fig. 8

You open the card file in input mode because it is to be read and the amend file in output mode because it is going to be created or written.

```
AB-READ.
     READ CARD-IN AT END GO TO ZZ-END.
     MOVE SPACES TO AMEND-REC-IA.
```

This clears the output record area to spaces. Remember AMEND–REC–IA shares the same store with AMEND–REC–D.

```
IF   CARD-TYPE = "I" OR
     CARD-TYPE = "A" OR
     CARD-TYPE = "D" NEXT SENTENCE
ELSE
     GO TO XX-INVALID.
MOVE CARD-TYPE TO AMEND-TYPE-IA.
```

This checks that card type is valid. If it is not, control passes to XX–INVALID. The type is then moved to the output record.

```
IF CARD-AREA NOT NUMERIC GO TO XX-INVALID.
IF CARD-AREA < 1 OR
   CARD-AREA > 4 GO TO XX-INVALID.
```

The area must be checked for 1, 2, 3 or 4. The IF statement does this using a compound relation test.

```
MOVE CARD-GROUP TO AMEND-GROUP-IA.
IF CARD-TYPE = "D"
     MOVE "DELETE" TO AMEND-DEL
     GO TO FF-WRITE-D.
```

The AREA and CODE can be moved as a group to the output record.
If the type is D, 'DELETE' is to be moved to the AMEND–DEL field on
the AMEND–REC–D record. Control is then passed to paragraph FF–
WRITE–D.

```
IF CARD-AREA = 1 MOVE "SOUTHERN" TO AMEND-NAME
                 GO TO CC-TOTAL.
IF CARD-AREA = 2 MOVE "EASTERN" TO AMEND-NAME
                 GO TO CC-TOTAL.
IF CARD-AREA = 3 MOVE "NORTHERN" TO AMEND-NAME
                 GO TO CC-TOTAL.
IF CARD-AREA = 4 MOVE "WESTERN" TO AMEND-NAME
                 GO TO CC-TOTAL.
```

The correct area name is moved to the AMEND–NAME field on the
AMEND–REC–IA record.

```
CC-TOTAL.
     ADD CARD-TOTAL-1    CARD-TOTAL-2 GIVING AMEND-TOTAL.
```

The two totals on the card record are added together and placed in the
AMEND–TOTAL field. Notice that this field is a computational synchronised field.

All fields have now been set up in the output record buffer. AMEND–
REC–IA has had the type, group, name and total moved to it, it is now
ready to be written to the output file. The verb is WRITE and it commits
the content of the record to the output media – in this case a
disc.

```
WRITE record name.
```

```
DD-WRITE-IA.
     WRITE AMEND-REC-IA.
     GO TO AB-READ.
```

The content of that record has now been written to the file stated in the
SELECT . . . ASSIGN statement. The record-name must be the 01 level
name and cannot be any other level. Always create the whole record
buffer before WRITEing it. You then return to read another record.

But if the record type is D we do not write an AMEND–REC–IA record;
instead we write an AMEND–REC–D record. Control branches to FF–
WRITE–D if the type is D. At this point all the fields have been moved to
AMEND–REC–D, the type, group and DELETE. Remember AMEND–REC–D
and AMEND–REC–IA name the same area of store, so in moving the type
to AMEND–TYPE–IA you are also moving it to AMEND–TYPE–D.

```
FF-WRITE-D.
    WRITE AMEND-REC-D.
    GO TO AB-READ.
```

The record that you want to write is the shorter of the two. The record name or 01 level is AMEND–REC–D.

This completes the main logic of the program:

```
XX-INVALID.
    DISPLAY CARD-REC.
    GO TO AB-READ.
```

If the record is invalid the content of the record is displayed, control then returns to the READ.

```
ZZ-END.
    CLOSE CARD-IN AMEND-OUT.
    STOP RUN.
```

Both files can be closed in one statement. The program execution is then stopped.

This is a simple example of validating an input sequential file and creating a valid output sequential file.

A file must be SELECTed in the environment division and must be described in the file section. There must be an 01 level to describe each record format in a file. The largest record described determines the size of the record buffer allocated. When a record is read it is placed in the record buffer from left to right. A record is recorded by using a WRITE statement. The content of the record name stated is written to the file selected in the environment division. The record buffer must be complete before a WRITE is issued. Files must be opened before they can be written or read, the mode of use must be stated when the file is opened. The files must be closed when processing is complete, usually at the end of the program. The close statement does not state the mode of the file.

Updating a file

Many of the large data files used in a computer system will be master files: files with 'master' information, account files with details of each account holder, or pay master file with details of each employee. These files must be kept up to date, new accounts added, details of account holders changed, account holders who close their account deleted, etc. Depending on the importance of this up-to-dateness, the master file will be *updated* daily, weekly or monthly. The file with the update information is called an *amendment file* and contains information about new, changed or closed accounts. Fig. 9 shows a system diagram of a weekly master update. (A system diagram is a high level diagram showing the sequence that programs are run within a system and the files that are input and output to those programs.)

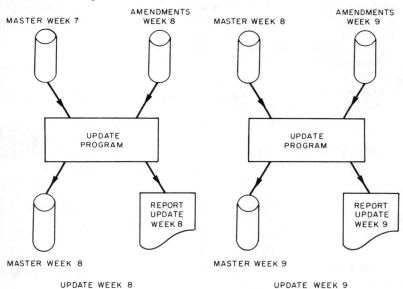

Update Diagram

Fig. 9

The first figure shows a week 7 master file being read with amendments for the current week 8. The master file is copied to an output file incorporating the amendments. A report is produced to list the actioned amendments and any amendments that could not be actioned. The second figure shows the same process, but this time the output master from week 8 is the input and the amendments are for current week 9. The input master must have the same record format as the output master because the output master becomes next week's input master. The data on the master and amendment file must be in the same sequence, e.g. the account number of an account file will be the key to that sequence. Data on master files is usually held in ascending sequence and the amendment file must be sorted into the same ascending key sequence. This method of copying and updating is called *copy updating*. It is a secure way to update, because data is not being destroyed as the input master is unchanged. If there is a problem with the output master, say the program has gone wrong, then it is easy to recover from that problem because the input is safe. It is common to save the three most recent versions of a master file for security (these are the son, father and grandfather master files). These versions are more commonly called *generations* as the terms son, father and grandfather imply.

Here is a simple update program specification. You will recognise the amendment file, it was validated and created in the previous example program.

Master file – held on disc, input name DA01, output name DA02.
Record contains – GROUP   5 alphanumeric
                 NAME   14 alphanumeric
                 TOTAL   6 numeric binary synchronised.
Amendment file – held on disc, name DA03. It contains 2 record types.
        – (1) TYPE   1 alphanumeric – I or A
               GROUP   5 alphanumeric
               NAME   14 alphanumeric
               TOTAL   6 numeric binary synchronised
        – (2) TYPE   1 alphanumeric – D
               GROUP   5 alphanumeric
               DELETE   6 alphanumeric

TYPE I is a new or insert record. TYPE A is an amendment record. TYPE D is a delete record.

The master and amendment files are both in ascending GROUP sequence. This is the key field used to match the files. Read a record from both files.

1 If the master record has no matching amendment record, copy the input master record to the output master, then read another master record.
2 If the amendment record has no matching master record then the amendment should be Type I. If it is not, display INVALID RECORD and return to read another amendment record. If it is a Type I, then an output master is to be created and written using amendment details. Return to read another amendment record.
3 If the amendment and master records match and the amendment is Type I, display INVALID RECORD and return to read both files. You cannot insert a new record when a record with the same key already exists. If the amendment Type is D, then display both fields in the record and return to read both files. To delete the record it is *not* copied to the new output master. If the amendment Type is A then add the amendment total to the master record total and write the updated record. Return to read both files.

The most common problem with updates is when to stop the run. If the amendment file finishes first then the remaining master records must be copied across. If the master file finishes first then the remaining amendment records must be processed – these may be new insert records at the end of the file. The program is complete when both files have come to the end.

Fig. 10 shows a flow diagram of the program. We are able to deal with the end of file situations. When discussing the collating-sequence the figurative constant HIGH–VALUES was said to be the highest value one character could hold. This is useful, as it will always compare as greater than any other value. We use this to drive our end of file logic. If the amendment file ends, move HIGH–VALUES to the amendment key field – this forces key comparisons through the MASTER–ALONE path. If the master file ends move HIGH–VALUES to the master key field; this forces key comparisons through the AMEND–ALONE path. Only when the keys are equal and equal to HIGH–VALUES have all the records on both the files been processed. Here is the coded program.

```
ENVIRONMENT DIVISION.
FILE-CONTROL.
      SELECT MAST-IN ASSIGN MS DA01.
      SELECT AMEND-IN ASSIGN MS DA03.
      SELECT MAST-OUT ASSIGN MS DA02.
```

All three files must be SELECTed.

```
DATA DIVISION.
FILE SECTION.
FD MAST-IN.
01 MAST-IN-REC.
      03 MAST-IN-GROUP    PIC X(5).
      03 MAST-IN-NAME     PIC X(14).
      03 MAST-IN-TOTAL    PIC 9(6) COMP SYNC RIGHT.

FD AMEND-IN.
01 AMEND-REC.
      03 AMEND-TYPE       PIC X.
      03 AMEND-GROUP      PIC X(5).
      03 AMEND-NAME       PIC X(14).
      03 AMEND-TOTAL      PIC 9(6) COMP SYNC RIGHT.
01 AMEND-REC-D.
      03 FILLER           PIC X(6).
      03 AMEND-DEL        PIC X(6).
```

The type and group on the D type record need not be pictured because they are described on the other amend record. Remember, they share the same piece of store and only one record can be in that store at a time.

80   *Computer Programming in COBOL*

Copy-Update Flowchart

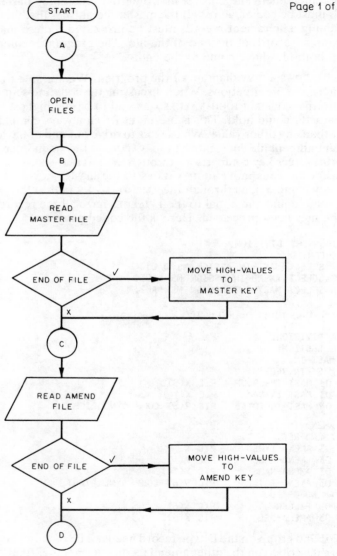

Fig. 10a

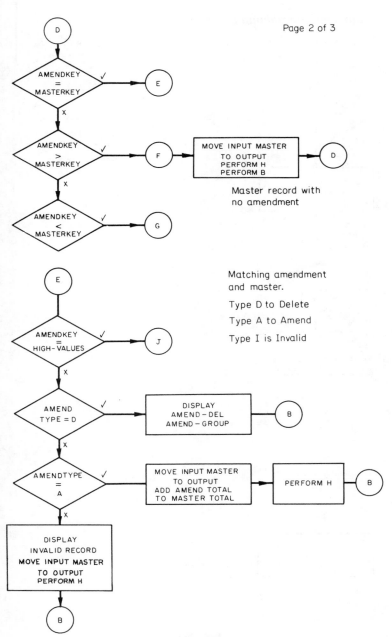

Master record with
no amendment

Matching amendment
and master.

Type D to Delete

Type A to Amend

Type I is Invalid

Fig. 10b

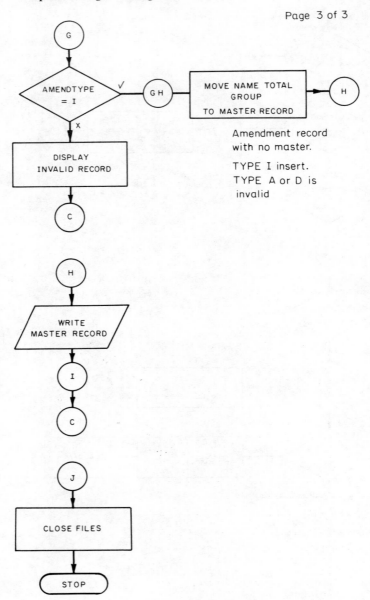

Amendment record
with no master.

TYPE I insert.
TYPE A or D is
invalid

Fig. 10c

```
FD MAST-OUT.
01 MAST-OUT-REC.
    03 MAST-OUT-GROUP PIC X(5).
    03 MAST-OUT-NAME  PIC X(14).
    03 MAST-OUT-TOTAL PIC 9(6) COMP SYNC RIGHT.
```

The MAST–IN and MAST–OUT files have been described in the same way because they describe different versions of the same master file.

```
PROCEDURE DIVISION.
AA-START.
      OPEN INPUT MAST-IN AMEND-IN.
      OPEN OUTPUT MAST-OUT.

BB-READ-MAST.
      READ MAST-IN AT END
            MOVE HIGH-VALUES TO MAST-IN-GROUP.

CC-READ-AMEND.
      READ AMEND-IN AT END
            MOVE HIGH-VALUES TO AMEND-GROUP.
```

When the AMEND file is READ you do not know whether a type A, I or D record has been placed in the record buffer. This will be determined later in the program.

```
DD-COMPARE.
      IF AMEND-GROUP = MAST-IN-GROUP
         GO TO EE-EQUAL.
      IF AMEND-GROUP > MAST-IN-GROUP
         GO TO FF-MAST-ALONE.
      IF AMEND-GROUP < MAST-IN-GROUP
         GO TO GG-AMEND-ALONE.
*        COMPARE KEY FIELDS TO DETERMINE ACTION

EE-EQUAL.
      IF AMEND-GROUP = HIGH-VALUES GO TO JJ-END.
      IF AMEND-TYPE = "D" GO TO EF-DELETE.
      IF AMEND-TYPE = "A" GO TO EG-AMEND.
      DISPLAY "INVALID RECORD".
      MOVE MAST-IN-REC TO MAST-OUT-REC.
      PERFORM HH-WRITE.
      GO TO BB-READ-MAST.
```

A type I would be invalid, you cannot insert a record when one already exists on the file with the same key value.

```
EG-AMEND.
      MOVE MAST-IN-REC TO MAST-OUT-REC.
      ADD AMEND-TOTAL TO MAST-OUT-TOTAL.
      PERFORM HH-WRITE.
      GO TO BB-READ-MAST.
*        TYPE A AMENDS A RECORD
```

The input record is copied across to the output record and the total is incremented, control then returns to read the master file.

```
EF-DELETE.
      DISPLAY AMEND-DEL AMEND-GROUP.
      GO TO BB-READ-MAST.
*     TYPE D DELETES A RECORD
```

The input master record is not copied to the output file, this effectively deletes the record.

```
FF-MAST-ALONE.
      MOVE MAST-IN-REC TO MAST-OUT-REC.
      PERFORM HH-WRITE.
      PERFORM BB-READ-MAST.
      GO TO DD-COMPARE.
*     NO AMENDMENT AND THE MASTER IS COPIED UNCHANGED
```

There is no amendment for this record: the input master record is copied to the output master file: control returns to read a master record.

```
GG-AMEND-ALONE.
      IF AMEND-TYPE = "I" GO TO GH-INSERT.
      DISPLAY "INVALID RECORD".
      GO TO CC-READ-AMEND.
*     INVALID TYPE I
  GH-INSERT.
      MOVE AMEND-GROUP TO MAST-OUT-GROUP.
      MOVE AMEND-NAME TO MAST-OUT-NAME.
      MOVE AMEND-TOTAL TO MAST-OUT-TOTAL.
*     CREATE A NEW MASTER
  HH-WRITE.
      WRITE MAST-OUT-REC.
  II-RETURN.
      GO TO CC-READ-AMEND.
```

If the amend key is lower than the master key then the type should be I. If it is not an I then the record is invalid. The output master record is created from the amend record and then written. Control returns to read an amendment record.

```
JJ-END.
      CLOSE MAST-IN AMEND-IN MAST-OUT.
  STOP RUN.
```

The files are closed and the program run stopped.

Blocking

When looking at the READ and WRITE statement it would appear that when a READ is executed the software goes to the media, say magnetic tape, gets a record and places it in the input record buffer; that when a WRITE is executed the content of the record is copied on to the magnetic tape at that moment. It is easy to see that this READing and WRITEing small pieces of data would be like playing a tape recorder one note at a time, would cause excessive wear and be time-consuming. To combat this, records are BLOCKed. Commonly, blocks will be about 2000 bytes long, so our AMEND—OUT file may be blocked in 80 record blocks. Now, when you say READ, a whole block will be read into store and only the first record placed in the record buffer, subsequent reads will get the next record from the block in store. When all the stored records have been read another block will be read and so on. When you say WRITE the record is placed in the block store area which is called a block buffer. Only when the buffer is full will the block be written, unless the file is closed and then a part-filled block will be written. This block buffer concept should not affect the programmer, the buffer area is not part of your program. Some dialects of COBOL ask you to state the block size in the FD description.

```
FD AMEND-OUT
    BLOCK CONTAINS 80 RECORDS.

FD MAST-FILE
    BLOCK CONTAINS 2048 CHARACTERS.
```

Notice that the full stop appears once, at the end of the BLOCK CONTAINS clause, which is the last in these FD statements.

Sequential file handling exercises

1 There are three errors in the following coding, what are they?

```
FD IN-FILE.
01 IN-REC.
    .
    .
    .
FD OUT-FILE.
01 OUT-REC.
    .
    .
    .
PROCEDURE DIVISION.
    .
    .
    OPEN INPUT IN-FILE.
    OPEN OUTPUT OUT-FILE.
    .
    .
    .
```

```
READ OUT-FILE AT END ...
   .
   .
   .
WRITE IN-REC.
   .
   .
   .
READ IN-REC AT END ...
```

2 Write the FD for this file with 3 record types.

File-name MAT–FILE.

(a)	Record type	1 character alphanumeric.
	Area	20 characters alphanumeric.
	Number	3 packed decimal digits.
(b)	Record type	1 character alphanumeric.
	Area	20 characters alphanumeric.
	Account code	6 digits numeric display.
(c)	Record type	1 character alphanumeric.
	Address	60 characters alphanumeric.

3 Write the necessary statements to output the three different records in question 2.

4 Write the following COBOL program.

  (i) Program name EX01.

  (ii) (a) Input File, name MT01, sequential magnetic tape file.

Input record.	
Personnel number	6 numeric display.
Name	20 alphanumeric characters.
Department	2 numeric display.
Unit	2 numeric display.
Years' Service	2 numeric display.
Date joined	6 numeric display (YYMMDD).
Grade code	3 alphanumeric characters.

  (b) Output File, name DA02, sequential disc file.

Output record.	
Personnel number	6 numeric display.
Name	20 alphanumeric characters.
Grade code	3 alphanumeric characters.
Year joined	2 numeric digits (YY).

(c) Output File named DA03, sequential disc file.
Output record.

Personnel number	6 numeric display.
Department	2 numeric display.
Unit	2 numeric display.
Years' service	2 numeric display.

(iii) Processing

(a) Read every record on the input MT01 file, create records to be output to the two output files.

To create a record for DA02, move the personnel number, name, grade code and the first two digits of the date joined field.

To create a record for DA03, move personnel number, department, unit and years' service. Write both records and return to read the input file.

(b) Maintain two counts, one for every record read and one for every record written to the output DA03 file.

(c) At the end of the input file, close the files and stop the run.

9

Table Handling

Occurs

You have learned that data is described in the data division and that each item or elementary field is given a PICTURE.

A table is a list of like items and in COBOL terms it means that each item in the table has the *same* PICTURE. Let us take a table which will hold six names each four characters long.

```
01  W-LIST.
    03  W-NAME-1          PIC  X(4).
    03  W-NAME-2          PIC  X(4).
    03  W-NAME-3          PIC  X(4).
    03  W-NAME-4          PIC  X(4).
    03  W-NAME-5          PIC  X(4).
    03  W-NAME-6          PIC  X(4).
```

W-LIST is 24 characters long, each name has a data-name and PICTURE. There is a shorter way of writing this using the OCCURS clause.

```
level-number    data-name   picture   clause   OCCURS   integer
                                                TIMES.
01  W-LIST.
    03  W-NAME             PIC  X(4)  OCCURS  6  TIMES.
```

An OCCURS clause can be used anywhere in the data division but not on an 01 level: it may not have a value clause.

In this example W-LIST is 24 characters long, W-NAME is 4 characters long and there are 6 of them. They occupy contiguous areas of store. You have given 6 areas the same name, W-NAME, but you must name each item uniquely, according to the rules of COBOL. This problem is overcome by using a *subscript* or occurrence number to modify the data-name. If you want to move JACK to the first name:

```
MOVE "JACK" TO W-NAME (1).
```

Following the data-name the subscript of 1 is held in brackets.

```
MOVE "JEAN" TO W-NAME (4).
```

will move JEAN to the fourth name. The brackets must contain a positive numeric literal or a data-name describing a positive numeric item.

```
MOVE "JANE" TO W-NAME (W-NUM).
```

Where W-NUM contains the value 2 then JANE will be moved to the second name.

Loops

Let us look at a more complex practical example: a file consisting of hundreds of records containing two items, a month number (01–12) and an amount of money. Twelve totals are to be accumulated and displayed at the end of the program.

All money on records with the month 01 is to be accumulated into the first total, money on records with the month 02 is to be accumulated into the second total and so on.

```
FILE SECTION.
FD IN-FILE.
01 IN-REC.
     03 IN-MONTH          PIC 99.
     03 IN-AMOUNT         PIC 9(6)V99 COMP SYNC RIGHT.
   .
   .
   .
WORKING-STORAGE SECTION.
01 W-TOTALS.
     03 W-MONTH-TOT       PIC 9(8)V99 COMP SYNC RIGHT
                          OCCURS 12.
```

W-TOTALS contains fields each able to hold one month's total.

```
PROCEDURE DIVISION.
   .
     INITIALISE W-TOTALS.
```

In common with most totalling fields, these twelve totals must start with the value zero.

INITIALISE will set each of the numeric totals to binary zero. If you said MOVE ZERO TO W-TOTALS the area would contain display zeros which would be incorrect.

```
        .
        .
BB-READ.
        READ IN-FILE AT END
                    GO TO ZZ-END.
```

When a record has been read, the value of IN–MONTH will determine
which of the twelve w–MONTH–TOT fields IN–AMOUNT is to be added to.

```
ADD IN-AMOUNT TO W-MONTH-TOT ...
```

That is the statement you would use, but you must state which
w–MONTH–TOT. IN–MONTH holds that information, it is numeric and
can be used as a subscript.

```
ADD IN-AMOUNT TO W-MONTH-TOT (IN-MONTH).
```

This is the correct statement. If IN–MONTH contains 04 then IN–AMOUNT
will be added to the fourth occurrence of w–MONTH–TOT. It is essential
that the subscript contains a valid value. If IN–MONTH contained 00 or a
value greater than 12 then it would be OUT OF RANGE. This will cause
errors in your program.

```
GO TO BB-READ.
```

Return to read another record. This loop will continue until the end of
file is reached and all the records have been processed. ZZ–END is the
paragraph where you have to display each of the monthly totals
separately.
   If you say:

```
ZZ-END.
        DISPLAY W-MONTH-TOT (1).
        DISPLAY W-MONTH-TOT (2).
                .
                .
```

and so on, it would be quite correct.
   If the table had been 100 items long, then that coding would take a
long time to write. Instead we can use a subscript.

```
DISPLAY W-MONTH-TOT (?).
```

This is correct but the subscript has to vary from 1 to 12 and we must
execute the code 12 times. For this we set up a loop with a variable
subscript, named w–SUB, in working-storage.

```
01 W-SUB                    PIC 99.
  .
  .
  .
ZZ-END.
    MOVE ZERO TO W-SUB.
```

```
ZZ-DISPLAY.
     ADD 1 TO W-SUB.
     DISPLAY W-MONTH-TOT (W-SUB).
     IF W-SUB < 12
         GO TO ZZ-DISPLAY.
ZZ-FINAL.
     CLOSE IN-FILE.
     STOP RUN.
```

The field w–sub must be pictured to hold the largest variable value, in this case 12. w–sub is zeroised then zz–display starts the loop.

The first time around the loop w–sub will be 1 and the first total will be displayed. The second time it will be 2 and so on until the twelfth and final total has been displayed. The if tests for the value 12. If w–sub is 12 then all the totals have been displayed and zz–final is executed. Another way of writing the same loop is:

```
ZZ-END.
     MOVE 1 TO W-SUB.
ZZ-DISPLAY.
     DISPLAY W-MONTH-TOT (W-SUB).
     IF W-SUB = 12 GO TO ZZ-FINAL.
     ADD 1 TO W-SUB.
     GO TO ZZ-DISPLAY.
ZZ-FINAL.
     .
     .
     .
```

Perform . . .

In both cases zz–display is a common piece of code – it is used 12 times. You learned in chapter 7 that the verb perform can be used when dealing with common code. We now examine three extensions to the perform verb.

The first type of Perform

```
PERFORM procedure-name-1 [THRU procedure-name-2]
  ⎰integer  ⎱  TIMES.
  ⎱identifier⎰
ZZ-END.
     MOVE ZERO TO W-SUB.
     PERFORM ZZ-DISPLAY 12 TIMES.
     CLOSE IN-FILE.
     STOP RUN.
ZZ-DISPLAY.
     ADD 1 TO W-SUB.
     DISPLAY W-MONTH-TOT (W-SUB).
```

Again the subscript is zeroised at the start of the loop. ZZ–DISPLAY will be PERFORMED 12 times each time W–SUB will be incremented by 1 using the ADD statement. When the code has been PERFORMED 12 times control passes to the statement after the PERFORM, CLOSE IN–FILE.

The second type of Perform

```
PERFORM procedure-name-1 [THRU procedure-name-2]
        UNTIL condition.
ZZ-END.
     MOVE ZERO TO W-SUB.
     PERFORM ZZ-DISPLAY
          UNTIL W-SUB = 12.
     CLOSE IN-FILE.
     STOP RUN.
ZZ-DISPLAY.
     ADD 1 TO W-SUB.
     DISPLAY W-MONTH (W-SUB).
```

The condition is any valid condition used in an IF verb. The condition is tested before the procedure is PERFORMED. Using the second PERFORM format again.

```
ZZ-END.
     MOVE 1 TO W-SUB.
     PERFORM ZZ-DISPLAY.
          UNTIL W-SUB > 12.
     CLOSE IN-FILE.
     STOP RUN.
ZZ-DISPLAY.
     DISPLAY W-MONTH-TOT (W-SUB).
     ADD 1 TO W-SUB.
```

W–SUB starts at 1, in order to perform the loop twelve times, the condition must be greater than 12 i.e.: 13.

The third type of Perform

```
PERFORM procedure-name-1 [THRU procedure-name-2]

        VARYING identifier-1 FROM  { identifier-2 }
                                   { literal-1    }

        BY { identifier-3 }  UNTIL condition.
           { literal-2    }
```

This copes with the loop and the varying of the subscript.

```
ZZ-END.
     PERFORM ZZ-DISPLAY
          VARYING W-SUB FROM 1 BY 1
               UNTIL W-SUB > 12.
```

```
        CLOSE IN-FILE.
        STOP RUN.
    ZZ-DISPLAY.
        DISPLAY W-MONTH-TOT (W-SUB).
```

The subscript w–SUB starts at 1, for every PERFORM it is incremented by 1, the condition is tested and if untrue the PERFORM takes place. Data-names may be used instead of literals.

You have seen many ways of doing the same piece of program, choose the method that you understand best and most readily fits the problem.

A subscript modifies a data-name described in the data division with an OCCURS clause. A subscript may be any literal or data-name containing a positive numeric value, the value must be in the range of the OCCURS clause.

An OCCURS clause may not be used on an 01 level and may not have a value clause, it may, however, have an 88 level condition-name. PERFORM is a useful verb to use in conjunction with a table, the various extensions of the PERFORM verb allow you to control the varying of the subscript and the loop in different ways.

Complex Occurs

Take the original table of names, for each name you now have an amount of savings.

```
01 W-LIST.
  03 W-SAVE OCCURS 6 TIMES.
        05  W-NAME          PIC X(4).
        05  W-AMOUNT        PIC 999V99.
```

This describes a group w–SAVE which OCCURS 6 times. The group has two fields, name and amount, the six groups occupy contiguous areas of store.

```
MOVE W-NAME (6) TO W-AREA.
ADD 10 TO W-AMOUNT (W-SUB).
```

The subscript is used in the same way but you can also reference the group.

```
MOVE W-SAVE (5) TO OUT-AREA.
```

The fifth occurrence of the group will be moved. So the OCCURS clause applies to the data-name which OCCURS and the underlying fields.

```
01 W-LIST.
    03 W-NAME          PIC X(4) OCCURS 6 TIMES.
    03 W-AMOUNT        PIC 999V99 OCCURS 6 TIMES.
```

This is valid but does not describe the same table as the previous example. Six names will occur followed by six amounts.

Multiple Occurs

Consider an hotel chain. It has hotels in 50 countries, in each country it has 30 areas, and has 10 hotels in each area. You are to PICTURE a table containing a total of single and double beds for each hotel in each area in each country.

```
01  W-HOTEL-BEDS.
      03  W-COUNTRY OCCURS 50 TIMES.
           05  W-AREA OCCURS 30 TIMES.
                07  W-HOTEL OCCURS 10 TIMES.
                     09  W-SINGLE          PIC 9(9).
                     09  W-DOUBLE          PIC 9(9).
```

Here you have described 15 000 hotels and each hotel has two bed types giving 30 000 totals.

To reference a country:

```
W-COUNTRY (SUB-1)
```

To reference an area:

```
W-AREA (SUB-1 SUB-2)
```

To reference an hotel:

```
W-HOTEL (SUB-1 SUB-2 SUB-3)
```

To add into the double bed total:

```
ADD TOTAL TO W-DOUBLE (SUB-1 SUB-2 SUB-3).
```

Each subscript modifies a level of this multiple table.

The first single bed in the table could be referenced:

```
W-SINGLE (1 1 1)
```

The last:

```
W-SINGLE (50 30 10)
```

There must be a space between each subscript. You are allowed a maximum of three multiple OCCURS.

Occurs . . . depending

Some tables vary in size and we are able to describe, in COBOL, this type of table.

```
level number data-name-1 picture clause OCCURS integer-1
                                 TO integer-2 TIMES DEPENDING
                                    ON data-name-2.
   01 WS-TABLE.
      03 WS-ITEM          PIC X(3) OCCURS
         10 TO 40 TIMES DEPENDING ON WS-NUM.
```

The range of OCCURS must be stated; 0 to 100 is a valid statement. Data-name-2 must be a numeric field. If you say:

```
MOVE WS-TABLE TO PR-AREA.
```

WS–NUM will determine how much of WS–TABLE will be moved. If WS–NUM contains 12, then 36 characters will be moved. If WS–NUM has an OUT OF RANGE value the whole of WS–TABLE will be moved. Any verb using a piece of data, with the OCCURS . . . DEPENDING clause, will take note of the depending data-name and act upon that variable sized data.

Table handling exercise

1 Write the data description for the following tables.

   (a) A table named WS–TAB1 which has 20 elements each of 3 digits numeric display.
   (b) A table named WS–TAB2 which has 40 elements each element has two fields, WS–NAM alphanumeric 20 characters, and WS–ADD, alphanumeric 60 characters.
   (c) A table named WS–TAB3 has 10 elements each 4 characters alphabetic followed by WS–TAB4 of 10 elements each of 6 packed decimal digits.
   (d) A table named WS–TAB5 has 20 to 100 elements each of 3 numeric display digits, WS–COUNT determines the size of the table.

2
```
   PARA-A.
      ADD 1 TO A-COUNT.
      MOVE "X" TO PR-A.
   PARA-B.
      MOVE IN-CODE (A-COUNT) TO PR-B.
```
   (a) Write a PERFORM to execute these paragraphs six times.
   (b) Write a PERFORM to execute these paragraphs six times with A–COUNT starting at 1 and ending at 6.

3 Using a PERFORM . . . VARYING statement write the correct coding for the following:

   An amount of money TAB–AMOUNT occurs 70 times. Add each of the 70 amounts to a field TOTAL–AMOUNT. Use the subscript SUB–AMT. Use the paragraph name ADD–PARA.

4 A bank has 50 branches, a branch has 2 managers, a manager has 4 staff. The staff field is six binary synchronised digits. Write the data division entry for this table.

5 Write a loop (do not use PERFORM) to execute this code 12 times. The subscript A–SUB to start at 20.

```
ADD A-COUNT (A-SUB) TO TOTAL.
MOVE A-COUNT (A-SUB) TO PR-A.
```

6 Write the following COBOL program:

   (i) Program name. EX02.

   (ii) (a) Input file, name MT01, sequential magnetic tape file.
        Input record.

| Product name | 11 alphanumeric characters. |

        The following two fields occur ten times.

| Product group | 2 alphanumeric characters. |
| Value of group sale | 8 numeric binary synchronised. |

       (b) Output file, name MT02, sequential magnetic tape file. This file has two record types A and Z each has the same format.
        Output record.

Record type	1 alphanumeric character.
Product name	11 alphanumeric characters.
Total product value	10 numeric binary synchronised.

  (iii) Processing:

       (a) Read every record on the MT01 file.
       (b) For every input record create an output record on the MT02 file. Accumulate each of the ten, value of group sale, fields and write that total to the output record as the total product value, the detail output record has a type of A.
       (c) At end of file write a final type Z record to the MT02 file. This record has Z in the type field, spaces in the name field and zeros in the total product field. Close files and stop run.

10

Printing

There is no point in having a computer system if it does not give useful information. This information usually comes on paper, e.g. as a printed report, pay slip, telephone bill or statistics. When producing printout from a program remember that the user needs to be able to understand it, and that clear presentation will help that understanding. This chapter is about the production of a clearly understood report.

A printout is an output file in COBOL. This means that environment and data division entries have to be written. Each printed line is a record and, like magnetic files, these records can have different formats. Each line or record will be of a fixed length and that line need not be completely filled with information – spaces are an important part of making the printed line readable. The width of the paper or record length varies: 120, 132 and 160 characters are the most common. 132 character lines are used in this chapter.

Editing picture clauses

In order to present printed details clearly you have to PICTURE the printed fields using some of the following clauses. These clauses are only valid with usage display picture clauses.

1 / solidus – this can be used in X or 9 PICTURES.

```
03  WS-A        PIC  XX/XX/XX.
03  WS-B        PIC  9(3)/99.

MOVE "123456" TO WS-A.        12/34/56
MOVE    647     TO WS-B.        006/47
```

The MOVE takes place ignoring the solidi, which are inserted afterwards.

2 B this can be used in X or 9 pictures – a space is inserted for every B.

```
03 WS-A          PIC XBXBXXX.
03 WS-B          PIC 99B99.
MOVE "ABCDE" TO WS-A.          A B CDE
MOVE 3715    TO WS-B.          37 15
```

3 , comma – this character is used with 9 pictures.

```
03 WS-A          PIC 99,999.
03 WS-B          PIC 9,999,999.
MOVE 1205 TO WS-A.          01,205
MOVE 1287964 TO WS-B.       1,287,964
```

The comma may be inserted anywhere in the field.

4 I any character – this can be used in X or 9 pictures. The character following the I will be inserted.

```
03 WS-A          PIC XXI-XXILX.
03 WS-B          PIC 9IBIR99.
03 WS-C          PIC XXIP(3)X.
03 WS-D          PIC 9(6).
03 WS-E          PIC 9(4)I.99.
MOVE "FGHKM" TO WS-A.      FG-HKLM
MOVE 238 TO WS-B.          2BR38
MOVE "KLM" TO WS-C.        KLPPPM
```

If ws–d contained an amount in pence, say 314722, and the print-out is to be in pounds and pence, a full stop will be inserted correctly.

```
MOVE WS-D TO WS-E.          3147.22
```

Notice that the insert characters occupy extra characters of store. ws–b in the last example occupies 5 characters of store.

5 . full stop – this character is used in 9 pictures. The decimal point in the sending field is aligned with the . (full stop) in the receiving field.

```
03 WS-A          PIC 9(4).99.
03 WS-B          PIC 9(4)V99 VALUE 1234.56.
03 WS-C          PIC 9(4) VALUE 7890.
03 WS-D          PIC 9(6) VALUE 214731.
MOVE WS-B TO WS-A.          1234.56
MOVE WS-C TO WS-A.          7890.00
MOVE WS-D TO WS-A.          4731.00
```

A full stop on its own is used when the sending field has a v. An I. is used when the sending field is a whole number and has no v.

6 z suppression of leading zeros – it replaces them by spaces. It can be used with 9 pictures.

```
03 WS-E              PIC Z(5)9.
03 WS-Z              PIC Z(4).
MOVE 000123 TO WS-E.               123
MOVE 5      TO WS-E.                 5
MOVE 131076 TO WS-E.            131076
MOVE ZERO   TO WS-E.                 0
MOVE ZERO   TO WS-Z.            ∧∧∧∧
```

The z can only suppress leading zeros. The whole field can be suppressed but leaving one 9 allows for a single zero to be printed if zero is moved. Another example:

```
03 WS-F              PIC Z(3)999.
MOVE 12    TO WS-F.               012
MOVE 82347 TO WS-F.             82347
MOVE 189   TO WS-F.               189
```

7 + and −, plus and minus can be used in a 9 pictures when the sending field is signed.

```
03 WS-K              PIC S9(4) VALUE 1234.
03 WS-L              PIC +9(4).
03 WS-M              PIC S9(3) VALUE −123.
03 WS-N              PIC −9(4).
MOVE WS-K TO WS-L.              +1234
MOVE WS-M TO WS-L.              −0123
MOVE WS-K TO WS-N.               1234
MOVE WS-M TO WS-N.              −0123
```

A picture with a + prints the sign + or −. A picture with a − prints the minus sign but prints a space for a positive value. The sign may be held at either end of the field.

```
PIC 9(4)−.              PIC 9(4)+.
```

8 CR and DB, credit and debit signs – used in 9 pictures when the sending field is signed.

```
03 WS-P              PIC 9(6) VALUE 123456.
03 WS-Q              PIC S9(6) VALUE −456789.
03 WS-R              PIC 9(6)CR.
03 WS-T              PIC 9(6)DB.
MOVE WS-P TO WS-R.             123456
MOVE WS-Q TO WS-R.             456789CR
MOVE WS-P TO WS-T.             123456
MOVE WS-Q TO WS-T.             456789DB
```

The CR and DB are only printed if a negative value is moved. Note that ws–p is unsigned and a positive value is assumed.

9 £ or $, pound or dollar sign – used in 9 PICTURES. This enables you to print a currency sign in front of an amount of money.

```
03  WS-P               PIC  9(4) VALUE      1234.
03  WS-Q               PIC  $9(4).
03  WS-R               PIC  9(4)V99 VALUE 1234.56.
03  WS-S               PIC  £9(4).99.
MOVE  WS-P TO WS-Q.            $1234
MOVE  WS-R TO WS-S.            £1234.56
MOVE  123 TO WS-Q.            $0123
```

Always remember that the move takes place regardless of the editing symbols. In the third example the zero after the dollar sign looks ugly. To improve the presentation a floating sign may be used.

10 £, $, + and − can all be used as floating symbols as well as a fixed symbol, previously explained.

```
03  WS-T             PIC  £(6)9.
03  WS-U             PIC  $(3)9.999.
03  WS-V             PIC  −(5)9.
03  WS-W             PIC  +(4)9.
MOVE  123    TO  WS-T.           £123
MOVE  9      TO  WS-T.            £9
MOVE  12345  TO  WS-T.          £12345
MOVE  1.174  TO  WS-U.          $1.174
MOVE  3215.5 TO  WS-U.        $215.500
MOVE  −123   TO  WS-V.           −123
MOVE  83145  TO  WS-V.          83145
MOVE  1234   TO  WS-W.          +1234
MOVE  −5     TO  WS-W.            −5
```

WS-U only has room for 3 integral digits and a $ sign.
Most of these editing symbols can be mixed in a single picture clause.
Here are some examples:

```
PIC  ZZ,ZZ9.99.
PIC  ££,££9.
PIC  ZZ9CR.
PIC  −(6)9.99.
PIC  ZZZ.ZZ.
PIC  £Z,ZZ9.99DB.
```

You cannot use an edited field in an arithmetic statement except as a GIVING identifier or a receiving field in COMPUTE. You cannot de-edit a field by moving it back to an unedited field.

Print files

Now you have seen the various extra clauses for picturing data let us look at a simple printed report. The layout of a page will often be described on lined paper describing the line (vertical) and the column (horizontal) for each detail record.

Report layout

```
        COLUMN
  LINE 1    2
    1                     10
                          MONTHLY SALES REPORT
    2                                                    40
                                                         PAGE Z9
    3
    4     3               12              22             35
          REP             UNITS           AMOUNT         AVERAGE
    5     2               13              21             38
    6     XX/XX           ZZ9             ££££9.99       9.99
    7
    8
```

Lines 1, 2 and 4 are *heading lines* and appear at the top of each page. Line 6 is a *detail line*, and is printed on alternate lines, e.g. lines 6, 8, 10. The last detail line is on line 60, then a new page is started. The three heading lines have fixed information except line 2, where the page number will change for each new page. Fixed values can be held in working-storage. (Remember a value clause may not be used in the file section.) The detail line will have values moved to it from the input detail file.

```
FILE-CONTROL.
    SELECT IN-DETAILS ASSIGN TO MT MT01.
    SELECT PR-FILE ASSIGN TO LP LP02.
```

The print and detail files must be selected. The program reads a simple file containing the details to be printed.

```
FILE SECTION.
FD IN-DETAILS.
01 DET-REC.
    03 DET-REP          PIC X(4).
    03 DET-UNIT         PIC 9(3).
    03 DET-AMT          PIC 9(4)V99.
```

The amount is in whole pence. By putting a v in the picture we can use it as a pound/pence field or dollar/cent field.

The detail line is described as a record.

```
FD PR-FILE.
01 PR-REC.
```

```
03 FILLER          PIC X.
03 PR-REP          PIC XX/XX.
03 FILLER          PIC X(6).
03 PR-UNIT         PIC ZZ9.
03 FILLER          PIC X(5).
03 PR-AMT          PIC £(4)9.99.
03 FILLER          PIC X(9).
03 PR-AVE          PIC 9.99.
03 FILLER          PIC X(91).
```

Filler is used to describe the spaces between fields. You must describe the line or record starting from column 1. This record has 41 columns of detail, followed by 91 spaces, to make it a 132-character long record. The record buffer will be 132 characters long.

Working-storage

```
01 WS-HEAD-1              PIC X(29) VALUE
"           MONTHLY SALES REPORT".
01 WS-HEAD-2.
   03 FILLER             PIC X(39) VALUE SPACES.
   03 FILLER             PIC X(5) VALUE "PAGE".
   03 WS-PAGE            PIC Z9.
01 WS-HEAD-4             PIC X(41) VALUE
"  REP        UNITS     AMOUNT      AVERAGE"
```

The three heading lines have been described in working-storage, the only field that will change is WS–PAGE; we need a page count for this. The program has to decide when the page is complete so we need a *line count*.

```
01 WS-PAGE-CNT           PIC 99 COMP-3.
01 WS-LINE-CNT           PIC 99 COMP SYNC RIGHT.
```

It is usually simplest to break down a heading line into sub-fields in order to describe it. Remember that FILLER names are useful if you do not wish to reference that field explicitly. You may use a value with a FILLER. Value spaces must be used for any blank fields.

Continuation lines

You may describe a long heading line with a single value clause.

```
01 WS-HEAD                PIC X(100) VALUE
   "THIS IS A VERY LONG VALUE CLAUSE
-  "IT NEEDS MORE THAN ONE LINE".
```

The first line has a quote to start it and you must use every column up to and including column 72. The second line has a hyphen in column 7 and another opening quote, the closing quote is only at the end of the literal. You may spread a literal over more than two lines. A hyphen must appear in column 7 of every literal continuation line. This is the only time that the continuation hyphen is recommended. It may be used to continue a COBOL word.

```
ADD A-COUNT B-COUNT 100 TO C-
COUNT.
```

This is valid, but very messy.

```
ADD A-COUNT B-COUNT 100 TO
    C-COUNT.
```

is the recommended way of spreading a COBOL statement over more than one line.

Write

A print file is very like any other file up to this point. The difference is in the formatting of the page. The program has to print headings at the top of the page and the program has to skip the blank lines. An extension of the WRITE statement is used to do this.

```
WRITE record-name  ⎰BEFORE⎱  ADVANCING
                   ⎱AFTER ⎰


⎰ ⎰identifier⎱        ⎱
⎰ ⎱  integer ⎰ [LINES]⎰
⎰      PAGE           ⎰
```

WRITE record-name is familiar, but you also have to say what vertical movement is required on the page. The BEFORE/AFTER clause is used for this. For example:

```
WRITE PR-REC AFTER 2.
WRITE PR-REC BEFORE 2.
```

You have a choice.

```
AFTER 2
      →   LINE 6
          LINE 7
      →   LINE 8       XXXXXX
```

If the printer is at line 6 vertical movement of 2 lines will take place and the line printed on line 8. The printer will stay at line 8 until the next write instruction to this file.

```
BEFORE 2
      →   LINE 6       XXXXXX
          LINE 7
      →   LINE 8
```

If the printer is at line 6, the line will be printed, then vertical movement of 2 lines will take place. The printer will stay at line 8 until the next write instruction to this file.

Do not mix AFTER and BEFORE instructions on the same file as this may result in overprinting. Further examples will use the AFTER option. The integer or identifier which follows the AFTER must be a positive numeric value. Zero will result in printing taking place with no vertical movement. AFTER PAGE, means line up the paper at the top (line 1) of the next page then print a line.

BEFORE PAGE, means print a line then position at line 1 of the next page.

Printing stationery is continuous with perforations to allow the paper to fold. A page can be any size, the common sizes are 60, 66 and 72 lines per page. Special stationery for invoices and payslips will have a different number of lines per page. 66 line pages are used in this chapter.

```
PROCEDURE DIVISION.
AA-START.
    OPEN INPUT IN-DETAILS.
    OPEN OUTPUT PR-FILE.
    MOVE ZERO TO WS-LINE-CNT WS-PAGE-CNT.
```

The files are opened; a print file is always an output file; the line and page counts are zeroised.

```
BB-HEADING.
    ADD 1 TO WS-PAGE-CNT.
    MOVE WS-PAGE-CNT TO WS-PAGE.
```

Increment the page count and move it to the heading line. You cannot use an edited field in an arithmetic statement. Note that WS-PAGE is edited with a Z.

```
    MOVE WS-HEAD-1 TO PR-REC.
    WRITE PR-REC AFTER PAGE.
```

The record buffer PR-REC is 132 characters long and may be used as the record name for all writes to the PR-FILE. Moving WS-HEAD-1 TO PR-REC is a group move, you are not destroying the detail PICTURE clauses. The content of PR-REC is then printed on line 1 of the first page.

```
    MOVE WS-HEAD-2 TO PR-REC.
    WRITE PR-REC AFTER 1.
    MOVE WS-HEAD-4 TO PR-REC.
    WRITE PR-REC AFTER 2.
    ADD 4 TO WS-LINE-CNT.
```

The first four lines have been printed, the line-count is incremented to reflect this.

```
CC-READ.
     READ IN-DETAILS AT END GO TO ZZ-END.
     MOVE SPACES TO PR-REC.
     MOVE DET-REP TO PR-REP.
     MOVE DET-UNIT TO PR-UNIT.
     MOVE DET-AMT TO PR-AMT.
     DIVIDE DET-UNIT INTO DET-AMT
             GIVING PR-AVE.
```

Having read a record the print record buffer is cleared to spaces. Three details are moved to the print detail record. To calculate the average the amount is divided by the units. Note that although the operands in an arithmetic statement must be unedited numeric, the identifier of the GIVING clause may be edited. The record is ready for printing.

```
     WRITE PR-REC AFTER 2.
     ADD 2 TO WS-LINE-CNT.
     IF WS-LINE-CNT = 60
         GO TO BB-HEADING.
     GO TO CC-READ.
```

The line count is incremented by 2. If the line count equals 60 the page is full and control passes to BB-HEADING where a new page is started. If the page is not full, control returns to CC-READ where another record is processed. The program ends like any other.

```
ZZ-END.
     CLOSE IN-DETAILS PR-FILE.
     STOP RUN.
```

Write . . . From

There is an extended form of the WRITE which can be used when writing any type of file, and is very useful for print files.

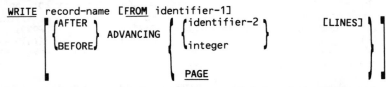

Identifier-1 is the data-name of an area in the data division that contains the record details.

The paragraph BB-HEADING could be written:

```
BB-HEADING.
        .
        .
        WRITE PR-REC FROM WS-HEAD-1 AFTER PAGE.
        WRITE PR-REC FROM WS-HEAD-2 AFTER 1.
```

```
WRITE PR-REC FROM WS-HEAD-4 AFTER 2.
          .
          .
          .
```

This is a short way of saying MOVE then WRITE. WS–HEAD–1 is moved to PR–REC then PR–REC is written.

Read . . . Into

```
READ file-name [INTO identifier]
          AT END imperative statements.
```

In the same way there is an extended form of the READ.

```
READ IN-DETAILS INTO WS-AREA
          AT END GO TO ZZ-END.
```

This is a shortened way of saying:

```
READ IN-DETAILS AT END GO TO ZZ-END.
MOVE DET-REC TO WS-AREA.
```

Printing exercises

1 MOVE A–FIELD TO B–FIELD.

	A–FIELD Picture	Content	B–FIELD Picture
(a)	X(6).	FLOWER	XXBXXXBX.
(b)	9(4).	2103	99/99.
(c)	99V99.	7248	99.99.
(d)	9999.	3182	99I.99.
(e)	9(6).	007431	Z(5)9.
(f)	999V9.	5465	999I.9.
(g)	999.	000	Z(3).
(h)	S9(4).	−1745	9(4)DB.
(i)	S9(4).	−0127	Z(3)9CR.
(j)	S9(3).	317	−999.
(k)	9(4)V99.	031750	£(4)9.99.
(l)	X(6).	AMERCA	XXXXIIXX.

What is the content of B–FIELD?

2 Describe this heading line in working-storage. Name it WS–HEAD.

ΔΔΔΔΔΔΔΔΔAREA REPORTΔΔΔΔΔΔΔΔΔΔΔΔΔΔΔΔΔΔΔΔΔΔΔΔΔΔΔΔΔΔΔΔΔΔΔSTATEMENT 12A

3 The record buffer for a print file is named PR–REC. Write the COBOL for the following:

   (a) Print the line at the top of the next page.
   (b) Leave 2 blank lines then print.
   (c) Print the line and leave 3 lines.

4 Given the following code:

```
01 WS-AMOUNT          PIC 9(6) COMP SYNC RIGHT.
01 WS-TOTAL           PIC 9(6) COMP SYNC RIGHT.
01 PR-TOTAL           PIC £(4)9I.99.
```

Which of the following statements are incorrect and why?

```
(a) ADD WS-AMOUNT TO PR-TOTAL.
(b) ADD WS-AMOUNT WS-TOTAL GIVING PR-TOTAL
(c) MOVE PR-TOTAL TO WS-TOTAL.
(d) SUBTRACT WS-TOTAL FROM WS-AMOUNT.
(e) MULTIPLY WS-AMOUNT BY PR-TOTAL.
```

5 Write the following COBOL program:

  (i) Program name. EX03.
  (ii) (a) Input File, name DA01, sequential disc file.
     Input record.

Account number	6 alphanumeric characters.
Account description	17 alphanumeric characters.
Credit limit	8 numeric binary synchronised.

  (b) Output file, name LP02, sequential printer file
     See attached print layout for record formats.

(iii) Processing

  (a) Read the DA01 file and print each detail record using the detail print line layout on line 5. Print the details with two blank lines between i.e.: 5, 8, 11, 14 etc.
  (b) The heading is to be printed on line 2 of each page.
  (c) The report is printed on special stationery 40 lines deep and 50 characters wide. The last detail line on a page is to be printed on line 35.

LP02 file layout

11

Indexed Sequential Files

In chapter 8 we saw how the most common file organisation, sequential, was created, read and updated. This chapter is about a file organisation called *indexed sequential*.

Take a dictionary that spreads across many volumes – the words are arranged in alphabetical order. If you want to reference the word SPROCKET you will first look at the spines of the books. Each spine will have the first letter of the first and last word held in that book e.g. A–D, E–G, S–Z. You will take the book S–Z, then look at the top of each page where the last word on that page will be written. SPUR at the top of the page will tell you that SPROCKET is on that page, you then read down the columns until the entry, SPROCKET, is found.

This process describes how you find something using indexes. The book spines were the first index, the highest level; the page tops were the second index, the lowest level. To create this file the information or data must be held in ascending sequence, it is sorted on the key which, in a dictionary, is the word. The words are written in columns on the pages and the last word on the page is written at the top of the page and so on until a book is full.

This indexed sequential organisation is very useful because a record can be accessed *randomly*. Unlike a sequential file where each record must be read in turn and records cannot be skipped over, random access allows you to read, write or change any record in the file without first accessing the preceding records.

In an indexed sequential file the data is held in one place and the indexes in another. Fig. 11 shows a simple diagram. The data is held in blocks and looks like a sequential file. Level 1 indexes are filled first. Take the first entry 1 15 that says 15 is the highest key in data block 1, 3 53 says 53 is the highest key in data block 3. When a Level 1 block is full

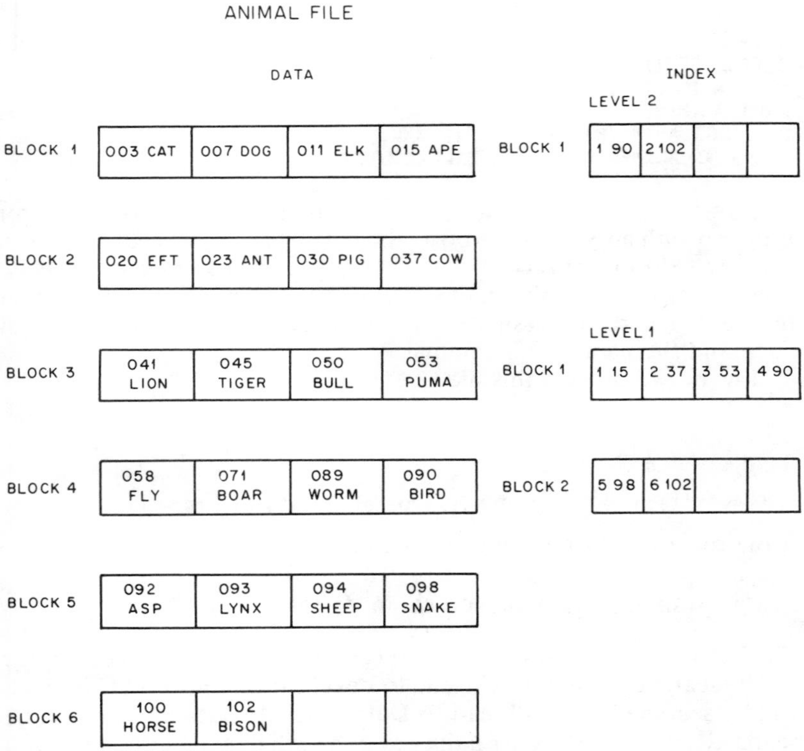

ANIMAL FILE

Indexed Sequential data and indexes

Fig. 11

a Level 2 entry is made. 1 90 says that the highest key of 90 is referenced in block 1 of Level 1 and so on. The indexes can grow to 3 Levels.

Still using Fig. 11 let us see what we can do with this data. The most important field is the key field which in this case is numeric and holds the animal code. We must tell the compiler where the key field is in the record and how it is PICTured. This is done in the SELECT and FD clauses. The file is called DA01. Indexed sequential files can only be held on disc.

```
FILE-CONTROL.
      SELECT ANIM-FILE ASSIGN TO MS DA01
             ORGANISATION IS INDEXED
             ACCESS MODE IS RANDOM
             RECORD KEY is ANIM-KEY.
```

```
       .
       .
FILE SECTION.
FD ANIM-FILE.
01 ANIM-REC.
    03 ANIM-KEY          PIC XXX.
    03 ANIM-NAME         PIC X(10).
```

The SELECT clause is extended to describe a file with ORGANISATION INDEXED with an ACCESS RANDOM mode. The RECORD key clause names the key field in the record buffer ANIM-KEY, whose picture must be non-numeric. Remember indexed sequential files can only be held on disc files. The record is simple, consisting of a key holding the animal code and the name of the animal.

How do we process this file?

Read

```
READ file-name INVALID KEY imperative statements
```

It the record with the key of 89 is to be read.

```
MOVE "089" TO ANIM-KEY.
READ ANIM-FILE INVALID KEY GO TO ZZ-ERROR.
```

The key required is moved to the record key field. The Level 2 index will be searched, and this will lead to Level 1 index block 1. This block will be searched and will lead to Data block 4. Data block 4 will be searched and the record with the key of 89 will be read into the record buffer ANIM—REC. The READ format is different because a RANDOM read cannot result in reading the END OF FILE, but the record being read may not be on the file. This is known as an INVALID KEY.

```
MOVE "043" TO ANIM-KEY.
READ ANIM-FILE INVALID KEY GO TO ZZ-ERROR.
```

The key of 43 is not on the file and control will pass to ZZ-ERROR. Unlike a sequential file we can update an indexed sequential file *in situ*, without copying it.

Write

To insert a new record the WRITE verb is used.

```
WRITE record-name INVALID KEY imperative statement
```

To insert key 099 with the name PONY on to the file.

```
MOVE "099" TO ANIM-KEY.
MOVE "PONY" TO ANIM-NAME.
WRITE ANIM-REC INVALID KEY GO TO XX-ERROR.
```

The record will be inserted into Data block 6, the block will now look like this.

```
099 PONY/100 HORSE/102 BISON
```

Note that the key sequence of the data is maintained.

You cannot insert a record with a key already on the file.

```
MOVE "030" TO ANIM-KEY.
MOVE "BAT" TO ANIM-NAME.
WRITE ANIM-REC INVALID KEY GO TO XX-ERROR.
```

This record will not be inserted, as duplicate keys are not allowed on an indexed sequential file. This will result in an INVALID KEY and control will pass to XX-ERROR.

Delete

If a record is to be taken off the file:

```
DELETE filename INVALID KEY imperative statement
```

To delete the record with key 11.

```
MOVE "011" TO ANIM-KEY.
DELETE ANIM-FILE INVALID KEY TO GO YY-ERROR.
```

The key 011 is deleted from Data block 1, leaving the block like this:

```
003CAT/007DOG/015APE/
```

An attempt to delete a record with a key not on the file:

```
MOVE "097" TO ANIM-KEY.
DELETE ANIM-FILE INVALID KEY GO TO YY-ERROR.
```

This will cause an INVALID KEY condition and control will pass to YY-ERROR.

Rewrite

If a record needs to be changed:

```
REWRITE record-name INVALID KEY imperative statement
```

The record with the key 58 is to be changed from FLY to FROG:

```
MOVE "058" TO ANIM-KEY.
READ ANIM-FILE AT END GO TO ZZ-ERROR.
```

```
MOVE "FROG" TO ANIM-NAME.
REWRITE ANIM-REC INVALID KEY GO TO VV-ERROR.
```

The record with key 058 is in Data block 4, leaving the block like this:

```
058FROG/71BOAR/89WORM/90BIRD/
```

It would be just as valid to write:

```
MOVE "058" TO ANIM-KEY.
MOVE "FROG" TO ANIM-NAME.
REWRITE ANIM-REC INVALID KEY GO TO VV-ERROR.
```

This will overwrite record 058 without first reading it. If the key to be overwritten does not exist this will cause an INVALID KEY and control will pass to VV-ERROR.

This ability to READ, WRITE, DELETE and REWRITE records randomly can reduce processing time and is a more flexible method of storing data.

In order to draw a comparison we will write the procedure code for the copy update problem in chapter 8. This time we need only two files as we are updating *in situ*. The master file is going to be input and output, read and written.

```
FILE-CONTROL.
        SELECT MAST-IN ASSIGN MS DAO1
                    ORGANISATION INDEXED
                    ACCESS RANDOM
                    RECORD KEY MAST-IN-GROUP.
        SELECT AMEND-IN ASSIGN MS DAO3.
            .
            .
            .
PROCEDURE DIVISION.
AA-START.
        OPEN I-O MAST-IN.
        OPEN INPUT AMEND-IN.
BB-READ-AMEND.
        READ AMEND-IN AT END GO TO JJ-END.
        IF AMEND-TYPE = "A" GO TO CC-AMEND.
        IF AMEND-TYPE = "I" GO TO DD-INSERT.
        IF AMEND-TYPE = "D" GO TO EE-DELETE.
CC-AMEND.
        MOVE AMEND-GROUP TO MAST-IN-GROUP.
        READ MAST-IN INVALID KEY
                        GO TO ZZ-ERROR.
        ADD AMEND-TOTAL TO MAST-IN-TOTAL.
        REWRITE MAST-IN-REC INVALID KEY
                        GO TO ZZ-ERROR.
        GO TO BB-READ-AMEND.
DD-INSERT.
        MOVE AMEND-GROUP TO MAST-IN-GROUP.
```

```
        MOVE AMEND-NAME TO MAST-IN-NAME.
        MOVE AMEND-TOTAL TO MAST-IN-TOTAL.
        WRITE MAST-IN-REC INVALID KEY
                        GO TO ZZ-ERROR.
        GO TO BB-READ-AMEND.
EE-DELETE.
        MOVE AMEND-GROUP TO MAST-IN-GROUP.
        DELETE MAST-IN INVALID KEY
                        GO TO ZZ-ERROR.
        DISPLAY AMEND-DEL AMEND-GROUP.
        GO TO BB-READ-AMEND.
ZZ-ERROR.
        DISPLAY "INVALID RECORD".
        GO TO BB-READ-AMEND.
JJ-END.
        CLOSE MAST-IN AMEND-IN.
        STOP RUN.
```

The end of the amendment file is the end of processing. Some records
will have been changed, inserted or deleted, the rest will be left
unchanged. The logic for an index-sequential file update is simpler
than for a sequential file update.

Overflow

From Fig. 11 (p. 109) you can see that if a record with a key of 21 is
inserted, data block 2 will not have room to store it. There are two
ways of coping with this. When the records are placed into the blocks
the blocks are not completely filled. This allows for some expansion
within a block. If, despite this spare capacity, the block is filled, then
an area of overflow is allocated. Any records unable to get into its
correct block will be stored in the overflow area for that block. The
overflow area is simply an empty data block at the end of the file. The
physical allocation and position of the overflow area varies on different
computers, however the concept remains the same.

Sequential access

An indexed sequential file may be read sequentially. The ACCESS
SEQUENTIAL statement should be made in the SELECT clause and the
procedure verbs are the same as for a sequential file:

```
SELECT MAST-FILE ASSIGN TO MS DA01
          ORGANISATION INDEXED
          ACCESS MODE SEQUENTIAL
          RECORD KEY MAST-IN.
```

There is an extra verb that can be used with an indexed sequential file accessed in sequential mode:

```
START filename KEY {IS >
                    IS =  } identifier
                    NOT <
            INVALID KEY imperative-statement
```

As the word START implies it starts access to the file.

```
MOVE "090" TO WS-KEY.
START MAST-FILE KEY = WS-KEY
        INVALID KEY GO TO ZZ-ERROR.
READ MAST-FILE AT END GO TO YY-END.
```

WS–KEY contains the value 90 so the indexes will be searched until the record with the key 90 is found. A READ following the START will then read the record with key 90 into the record buffer. Subsequent READS will access the records immediately following that record. Another START with a different key will then jump to that key and sequential reading can start from that point. This is sometimes called SKIP–SEQUENTIAL which nicely describes the process. Notice that the READ has an AT END clause because the file is being accessed sequentially.

Dynamic access

An indexed sequential file may be SELECTed with an *access mode dynamic*.

Dynamic mode allows you to access the file in *random* and *sequential* mode. All the file handling verbs may be used and records can be retrieved both RANDOMly and SEQUENTIAlly. To differentiate between the two methods of READing there is a different format of the READ verb which is used for sequential access in dynamic mode.

```
READ filename [NEXT RECORD]
        [INTO identifier]
        AT END imperative-statement
```

The word NEXT is used to indicate that the next sequential record is to be accessed. The AT END clause is used because the end of file might be detected.

```
SELECT MAST-FILE ASSIGN TO MS DAO1
        ORGANISATION INDEXED
        ACCESS MODE DYNAMIC
        RECORD KEY MAST-IN.
```

```
RANDOM-READ.
    MOVE AA-KEY TO MAST-IN.
    READ MAST-FILE
            INVALID KEY GO TO ZZ-ERROR
      .
      .
      .
SEQ-READ.
    READ MAST-FILE NEXT AT END GO TO YY-END.
      .
      .
      .
```

Indexed sequential exercises

1 Write the SELECT statement for the following:

A disc file named DA03 known as IS–FILE in COBOL.
The file has indexed sequential organisation and will be accessed randomly. The key field is IS–KEY.

2 Write the SELECT statement for the following:
  (a) A disc file named DA05 known as IN–FILE in COBOL.
      The file has indexed sequential organisation and will be accessed sequentially. The key field is IN–KEY.
  (b) Write the COBOL statements to open and read this file starting at key number 100, which is not the first record on the file.

3 Write the following COBOL program.

  (i) Program name. EX04.

  (ii) (a) Input file, name MT05, sequential magnetic tape file.
          Input record.

Catalogue number	8 alphanumeric characters.
Account number	6 numeric display digits.
Account name	60 alphanumeric characters.
Quantity ordered	6 numeric binary synchronised.

      (b) Input–Output File, name DA06, indexed sequential disc file.
          Record format – key field catalogue number.

Catalogue number	8 alphanumeric characters.
Price per item	7 packed numeric digits.
Quantity to date	8 numeric binary synchronised.

  (iii) Processing

      (a) Read every record on the input MT05 file; using the catalogue number access the indexed sequential DA06 file.

    (b) If the record is not on the file go to read another MT05 file.

    (c) If there is a record on the DA06 file, add the quantity ordered to the quantity to date field.

    (d) Multiply the updated quantity to date by the price per item and add the result to working storage total. This total is revenue to date.

    (e) Write the updated record to the DA06 file. If there is an invalid key return to read another record from MT05.

        If the record is written successfully return to read another record from MT05.

At the end of the MT05 file display the revenue to date field, close the files and stop the program.

12

Further Procedure Division

The important and most used COBOL facilities have been described in the previous chapters. This chapter looks at the rest of the procedure division verbs, some of which are advanced COBOL verbs. They will not be described in the same detail as previous verbs.

Accept and display

The verb DISPLAY is the partner to the verb ACCEPT. Both deal with low volume data. DISPLAY is a simple way of OUTPUTing messages. The message can be output to a printer, a video terminal, or more commonly to a journal file. A journal file is produced by the operating system and contains details of each program run.

```
DISPLAY {literal    }...
        {identifier }
```

The contents of an identifier and a literal may be displayed. By displaying more than one piece of data composite messages can be formed.

```
DISPLAY "TOTAL COUNT = " TOT-COUNT.
```

If TOT-COUNT contained 1234, the message

```
TOTAL COUNT = 1234
```

would be displayed.

ACCEPT is a verb used to INPUT small amounts of data.

```
ACCEPT identifier.
```

Say the data is held on a single card and contains the run week number, in columns 1 and 2 of the card are the digits 24.

```
01  WS-ACCEPT        PIC 99.
    .
    .
    .
    ACCEPT WS-ACCEPT.
```

The card will be read into the data field ws–ACCEPT. That field now contains the value 24.

This low-volume data is sometimes called *parameter information*. It can be made up of many fields and be as long as required. ACCEPT must not be used instead of a READ. There will usually be a maximum of one ACCEPT in a program. No SELECT, FD or OPEN is required.

Inspect

This verb is useful for validating data, and has two formats. One inspects the contents of a data area and counts the occurrence of a particular character or characters; the other inspects the contents of a data area replacing an occurrence of a particular character with another character.

Format:

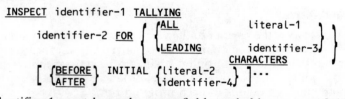

Identifier-1 must be a character field, probably a group field. Identifier-2 must be a numeric field which will hold the result of the count or tally.

```
MOVE ZERO TO WS-COUNT.
INSPECT WS-AREA TALLYING WS-COUNT
    FOR ALL "X".
```

The count will be incremented by 1 for every x found in ws–AREA. The inspect starts at the leftmost character and moves rightwards until the last character of ws–AREA has been inspected.

```
MOVE ZERO TO WS-COUNT.
INSPECT WS-AREA TALLYING WS-COUNT
    FOR LEADING "Y".
```

If ws–AREA has one or more ys in the leftmost positions then they are considered to be LEADING. If ws–AREA contained yyzzxx then ws–NUM would be incremented by 2.

```
MOVE ZERO TO WS-COUNT.
INSPECT WS-AREA TALLYING WS-COUNT
     FOR CHARACTERS
     BEFORE INITIAL "/".
```

If ws–area contained abcd13=t/17v then ws–num would be incremented by 8.

If the statement had been:

```
    .
    .
    .
    AFTER INITIAL "/".
```

then ws–num would have been incremented by 3.

Format 2:

```
INSPECT identifier-1 REPLACING
  ⎧⎧ ⎧ALL     ⎫ ⎧literal-1   ⎫      ⎧literal-2   ⎫ ⎫
  ⎨⎨ ⎨LEADING ⎬ ⎨identifier-2⎬  BY  ⎨identifier-3⎬ ⎬
  ⎩⎩ ⎩FIRST   ⎭ ⎩            ⎭      ⎩            ⎭ ⎭
                  CHARACTERS
     ⎡ ⎧BEFORE⎫            ⎧literal-3   ⎫ ⎤
     ⎢ ⎨AFTER ⎬ INITIAL    ⎨identifier-4⎬ ⎥
     ⎣ ⎩      ⎭            ⎩            ⎭ ⎦
```

Identifier-1 must be a character field probably a group field.

```
INSPECT WS-AREA REPLACING
     ALL "X" BY "Y".
```

If ws–area contained abxxt12x before, it will now contain abyyt12y.

```
INSPECT WS-AREA REPLACING
     LEADING "A" BY "D".
```

If ws–area contained atab12t before, it will now contain dtab12t. Only the leading a will be replaced by d.

```
INSPECT WS-AREA REPLACING
     LEADING "T" BY " ".
```

If ws–area contained btt12tba before, it will remain unchanged, as there are no leading ts.

```
INSPECT WS-AREA REPLACING
     FIRST "P" BY "K".
```

If ws–area contained abcp12p3 before, it will now contain abck12p3. Only the first p will be replaced.

```
INSPECT WS-AREA REPLACING
     FIRST "P" BY "K"
          AFTER "M".
```

If WS–AREA contained PABMTEPP before, it will contain PABMTEKP. The M will be found before the inspect starts to replace P by K.

If a program has a 9-character account code to validate, the account code must have 5 characters, a solidus and 3 characters in order to be valid.

```
INSPECT WS-ACCOUNT-CODE
    TALLYING WS-NUM1 FOR
        CHARACTERS BEFORE "/".

INSPECT WS-ACCOUNT-CODE
    TALLYING WS-NUM2 FOR
        CHARACTERS AFTER "/".

IF WS-NUM1 = 5 and WS-NUM2 = 3
    GO TO VALID-PARA.
```

String

This verb combines two or more pieces of data or literals, and places them in a receiving field.

```
STRING {identifier-1 }[ {identifier-2 }]....
       {literal-1    }  {literal-2    }
                                       {identifier-3}
           DELIMITED BY                {literal-3   }
                                       {SIZE        }

           INTO identifier-4.
```

All identifiers must be character fields.

```
WORKING-STORAGE SECTION.
     .
     .
     03 STREET-NO    PIC 99 VALUE 85.
     03 STREET-NAME  PIC X(20) VALUE "SOUTH ST".
     03 TOWN-NAME    PIC X(20) VALUE "TOYTOWN".
     .
     .
01 PRINT-REC        PIC X(60).
     .
     .
PROCEDURE DIVISION.
     .
     .
     .
     STRING STREET-NO STREET-NAME
         TOWN-NAME DELIMITED BY SIZE
             INTO PRINT-REC.
```

PRINT–REC will contain:

```
85SOUTH ST              TOYTOWN
```

The DELIMITED BY SIZE clause means move the whole of each of the sending fields to the receiving field PRINT–REC.

Let us improve on this:

```
STRING STREET-NO
          " "              DELIMITED BY SIZE
          STREET-NAME      DELIMITED BY " "
          " "              DELIMITED BY SIZE
          TOWN-NAME        DELIMITED BY SPACE
   INTO PRINT-REC.
```

PRINT–REC will contain:

```
85 SOUTH ST TOYTOWN
```

The street number and a space are moved by SIZE (the whole field), street name is moved until two spaces are found (the two spaces are not moved), a space is moved by size; town name is moved until a single space is found. Notice that in a STRING statement the figurative constant SPACE means a single space, and if more than one space is needed then they must be held in quotes.

Unstring

This verb breaks up a long character string into smaller data items.

```
UNSTRING identifier-1 [DELIMITED BY {identifier-2 }]
                                     {literal-1    }
    INTO identifier-3 [identifier-4] ...
```

All identifiers must be character fields.

```
WORKING-STORAGE SECTION.
01 WS-AREA              PIC X(6) VALUE "120382".
   .
   .
   03 WS-1             PIC XX.
   03 WS-2             PIC XX.
   03 WS-3             PIC XX.
   .
   .
PROCEDURE DIVISION.
   .
   .
   .
      UNSTRING WS-AREA
            INTO WS-1
                 WS-2
                 WS-3.
```

WS–1 is 2 characters long and will receive the first 2 characters from

WS–AREA and so on. After the unstring ws–1 contains 12, ws–2 contains 03, ws–3 contains 82.

```
01 WS-AREA              PIC X(10) VALUE "AB/12CD/XY".
   .
   .
   03 WS-1              PIC XXX.
   03 WS-2              PIC X(4).
   03 WS-3              PIC XX.
   .

PROCEDURE DIVISION.
   .
   .
   UNSTRING WS-AREA
            DELIMITED BY "/"
        INTO WS-1
             WS-2
             WS-3.
```

A move will take place from ws–area into ws–1 until a delimiter, /, is found. The / is not moved. A move into ws–2 moves the next piece of data up to but not including the next /.

ws–1 will contain AB△, ws–2 will contain 12CD, ws–3 will contain XY. The end of the sending data is also a delimiter. If the receiving field is larger than the data before the delimiter then the move takes place obeying the rules of numeric or non-numeric moves.

```
01 WS-AREA              PIC X(9) VALUE "*ATB123ZY".
   03 WS-1              PIC X(2).
   03 WS-3              PIC X(3).
   03 WS-2              PIC X(4).
PROCEDURE DIVISION.
   .
   .
   .
   UNSTRING WS-AREA
            DELIMITED BY "*"
        INTO WS-1
             WS-2
             WS-3
```

ws–1 will contain two spaces because a delimiter was found immediately, ws2 will contain ATB1, the next delimiter is the end of the data, therefore truncation will occur. ws–3 will not be changed because there was no ws–area data remaining to UNSTRING.

Copy and modules

This section describes two ways to borrow coding written by someone else.

Copy
This is a verb that instructs the compiler. The COPY verb may be used almost anywhere in your program.

```
COPY text-name.
```

If there is a long and complicated file description of a master file that is used in a number of programs the COPY statement may save you some work. One person codes the file description, using meaningful data-names.

```
01 MAST-REC.
    03 MAST-TYPE        PIC X.
    03 MAST-GROUP.
       05 MAST-AREA     PIC 9(4).
  .
  .
  .
  .
  .
```

That coding is punched on to cards and a piece of software will copy it on to a magnetic library file, a disc or magnetic tape. The COPY data will be given a filename, say COPYDATA. That coding is now stored and can be used by anyone who wants to use it.

```
FILE SECTION.
FD MAST-FILE.
COPY COPYDATA.
FD AMEND-FILE.
   .
   .
   .
```

You simply write COPY and the name of the COPY file in the correct place in your program. During compilation your source program is expanded with the COPY coding.

```
FILE SECTION.
FD MAST-FILE.
COPY COPYDATA.
01 MAST-REC.
    03 MAST-TYPE        PIC X.
    03 MAST-GROUP.
       05 MAST-AREA     PIC 9(4).
```

.
.
.
.

```
FD AMEND-FILE.
```

You must, of course, use the COPY coding data-names when writing procedure division statements.

Module calls

The COPY verb enables you to share pieces of coding. Program modules or subroutines enable you to borrow pieces of compiled logic.

Writing modular programs has three advantages. One is that a common piece of logic or module can be shared by many programs; two, that modules can be written in another language, say FORTRAN; three, splitting a large program into modules enables more programmers to develop the program and this can speed up program development.

The main program calls in the module when it wants to execute the modules code.

```
CALL [language-name] literal
    [USING identifier-1 [identifier-2]]...
```

Here is a main program and a module. The flowline describes the logic path.

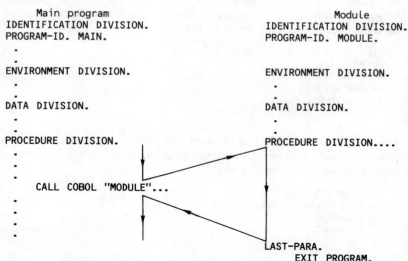

```
    Main program                              Module
IDENTIFICATION DIVISION.              IDENTIFICATION DIVISION.
PROGRAM-ID. MAIN.                     PROGRAM-ID. MODULE.
.
.
ENVIRONMENT DIVISION.                 ENVIRONMENT DIVISION.
.
.
DATA DIVISION.                        DATA DIVISION.
.
.
PROCEDURE DIVISION.                   PROCEDURE DIVISION....
.
.
.
      CALL COBOL "MODULE"...
.
.
.
.
                                      LAST-PARA.
                                          EXIT PROGRAM.
```

The language name, COBOL, describes the language of the module being called. The program-id of the module is used to CALL it, and this name must be in quotes: "MODULE".

A module is a complete program with all divisions coded. A module does not stop like a main program with a STOP RUN. The verb

```
EXIT PROGRAM.
```

is used, in a paragraph of its own, this verb returns control to the statement after the CALL in MAIN program. Module execution always starts at the first statement of the *procedure division* and ends at the *exit program* statement. A module may be called many times by a main program. Let's say a module calculates a salesman's bonus and also prints the bonus pay slip: it would therefore need a printfile. This file would have a SELECT, FD and the module would open it and close it. This open and close for a file 'owned' by the module can cause some logic problems. The execution of a module always starts at the *first* statement.

```
PROCEDURE DIVISION.
AA-START.
     OPEN OUTPUT BONUS-SLIPS.
BB-PROCESS.
```

If this were the coding then BONUS-SLIPS would be opened every time the module was used. The file only needs to be opened the first time the module is CALLed.

```
WORKING-STORAGE SECTION.
01 FIRST-FLAG        PIC X VALUE "1".
  .
  .
  .
  .
PROCEDURE DIVISION.
AA-START.
     IF FIRST-FLAG = "1"
         OPEN OUTPUT BONUS-SLIPS
         MOVE ZERO TO FIRST-FLAG.
BB-PROCESS.
```

The flag will only be set to 1 for the first call, after that it will be zero. The use of a flag solves this type of logic problem.

Linkage section

The main program will usually want to pass data to the module for the module to process. Having processed it, the module will want to return the results. This 'passing' data is often called *passing parameters*. The

data can be passed from any part of the data division of the main
program, but it is passed to and described in a special section called the
linkage section of the module.

```
        .
PROGRAM-ID. MAIN.
        .
        .
DATA DIVISION.
FILE SECTION.
FD FILEIN.
        .
        .
        03 SALES          PIC 9(6).
        03 TARGET         PIC 9(6).
        .
        .
WORKING-STORAGE SECTION.
        .
        .
01 QTR-MONTH-YR-FLAG PIC X.
01 BONUS             PIC 999V99.
        .
        .
PROCEDURE DIVISION.
        .
        .
        .
        CALL COBOL "MODULE" USING
        SALES TARGET
        QTR-MONTH-YR-FLAG BONUS.

PROGRAM-ID. MODULE.
        .
        .
DATA DIVISION.
FILE SECTION.
        .
        .
        .
WORKING-STORAGE SECTION.
        .
        .
        .
LINKAGE SECTION.
01 LINK-SALES        PIC 9(6).
01 LINK-TARGET       PIC 9(6).
01 LINK-FLAG         PIC X.
01 LINK-BONUS        PIC 999V99.
PROCEDURE DIVISION USING LINK-SALES LINK-TARGET
                        LINK-FLAG   LINK-BONUS.
```

```
AA-START.
        .
        .
        .
```

The main program has three data fields with information for the module: SALES, the salesman's achievement; TARGET, the salesman's target; and QTR–MONTH–YR–FLAG to indicate a monthly, quarterly or yearly bonus calculation. It also has one data field, BONUS, to receive results from the module.

Notice that these fields are in the file and working–storage sections. The module has the same four fields described in the LINKAGE section, they can have different data names but must have the same data descriptions. When the main program CALLs the module it must name the parameters with the USING clause.

```
CALL COBOL "MODULE" USING SALES TARGET
    QTR-MONTH-YR-FLAG BONUS.
```

All four fields must be named and the order must correspond with the procedure division statement in the module.

```
PROCEDURE DIVISION USING LINK-SALES LINK-TARGET
    LINK-FLAG LINK-BONUS.
```

When the CALL is executed the data passes from SALES to LINK–SALES, from TARGET to LINK–TARGET, and so on. This provides the module with data to process. When the exit program is executed the data will be passed from LINK–SALES to SALES, LINK–TARGET to TARGET, LINK–FLAG to QTR–MONTH–YR–FLAG and LINK–BONUS to BONUS. Control will pass to the statement after the CALL in the main program. BONUS now contains the calculated sum and the main program can use that data field.

Indexing and search

In this section we shall look at another way to write table handling codes (see chapter 9) and at a powerful verb that searches tables.

Indexing
A typical piece of coding using the OCCURS clause is:

```
01 WS-TAB1.
    03 WS-ITEM        PIC X(4) OCCURS 20.
01 WS-SUB             PIC 99 COMP SYNC RIGHT.
```

The table is a 4-character field with 20 occurrences; the subscript is a numeric field which is used to indicate which WS–ITEM is to be used, by modifying it.

```
WS-ITEM (WS-SUB).
```

Indexing offers an alternative way of doing this.

```
01 WS-TAB1.
   03 WS-ITEM          PIC X(4) OCCURS 20
                       INDEXED BY WS-IND1.
```

The OCCURS clause is extended by the statement INDEXED BY index-name.

The index-name is any valid data-name. In the example, WS–IND1 takes the place of WS–SUB. Unlike a subscript, WS–IND1 must not be described with a picture clause. When the INDEXED BY clause is used the index name is automatically described by the compiler – it is always a one word binary field. An index-name is used in the same way as a subscript:

```
WS-ITEM (WS-IND1)
```

but remember a subscript can be used with any table.

```
03 WS-TAB2          PIC 99 OCCURS 40.
   .
   .
   WS-TAB2 (WS-SUB).
```

This is not so with an index-name: this can only modify the table to which it belongs. Therefore the second table WS–TAB2 would look like this:

```
03 WS-TAB2          PIC 99 OCCURS 40
                    INDEXED BY WS-IND2.
   .
   .
   WS-TAB2 (WS-IND2)
```

It would have its own index-name to modify it.

A subscript is any numeric piece of data that contains a whole, positive value able to modify a table. An index-name is a piece of data which belongs to a specific table, is automatically described as a one word field, and contains a value which points to an item in a field, relative to the start of the table.

Take a simple table (Fig. 12):

```
03 WS-TAB           PIC X(4) OCCURS 3.
```

If the second occurrence was to be referenced then a subscript would contain 2, but an index-name would contain 5 because the second occurrence starts at the fifth character in the table. This is a simple way of looking at the difference between subscripts and indexes. Execution is generally quicker when an index-name is used.

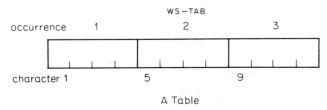

A Table

Fig. 12

How do we get the value 5 in the index-name? The verb SET is used.

SET $\begin{Bmatrix} \text{index-name-1} \\ \text{identifier-1} \end{Bmatrix}$..TO $\begin{Bmatrix} \text{identifier-2} \\ \text{integer-1} \end{Bmatrix}$

MOVE cannot be used with an index-name. SET must be used.

    SET WS-IND1 TO 6.

The correct pointer to the sixth occurrence will be generated for the table to which WS–IND1 belongs.

    SET WS-IND1 TO WS-NUM.

If WS–NUM contains 10 then the tenth occurrence pointer will be generated. Notice that the receiving field is first, unlike the MOVE verb:

    SET WS-NUM TO WS-IND1.

If WS–IND1 is referencing the nineteenth occurrence of its table then 19 will be placed in WS–NUM.

An index-name will have to vary in the same way as a subscript; the arithmetic verbs cannot be used with an index-name. Instead we use another form of the verb SET:

SET index-name $\begin{Bmatrix} \text{UP BY} \\ \text{DOWN BY} \end{Bmatrix}$ $\begin{Bmatrix} \text{identifier-1} \\ \text{integer-1} \end{Bmatrix}$

UP BY equates to ADD, DOWN BY equates to SUBTRACT.

    SET WS-IND1 UP BY 3.

If WS–IND1 was referencing item 7 it will now reference 10.

    SET WS—IND1 DOWN BY WS-NUM.

If WS–IND1 was referencing item 10 and WS–NUM contains 5, WS–IND1 will now reference item 5.

Let us compare a subscript loop with an index loop.

Subscript loop:

    03 WS-TAB   OCCURS 50.

```
      05  WS-A              PIC XX.
      05  WS-B              PIC 9(4).
01  WS-SUB                  PIC 99 COMP SYNC RIGHT.
.
.
      MOVE 1 TO WS-SUB.
A-PARA.
      MOVE WS-A (WS-SUB) TO PR-A.
      ADD WS-B (WS-SUB) TO WS-TOT.
      IF WS-SUB = 50 GO TO B-PARA.
      ADD 1 TO WS-SUB.
      GO TO A-PARA.
B-PARA.
```

Index loop:

```
      03  WS-TAB            OCCURS 50 INDEXED BY WS-IND.
          05  WS-A          PIC XX.
          05  WS-B          PIC 9(4).
.
.
      SET WS-IND TO 1.
A-PARA.
      MOVE WS-A (WS-IND) TO PR-A.
      ADD WS-B (WS-IND) TO WS-TOT.
      IF WS-IND = 50 GO TO B-PARA.
      SET WS-IND UP BY 1.
      GO TO A-PARA.
B-PARA.
```

You may use IF with an index-name, an index-name value will be
converted to an occurrence number before the test is made.

Search

This is a powerful verb that searches a table for an item. When the item
has been found or the table is exhausted then the SEARCH stops.

```
SEARCH identifier-1
       [AT END imperative statement]
                             {imperative statements}...
           WHEN condition-1  {NEXT SENTENCE     }
```

The table that we are going to search is full of animals and their daily
allowance of feed:

```
01  WS-CHART.
    03  WS-ZOO              OCCURS 150 INDEXED BY WS-INDA.
        05  WS-PET          PIC X(5).
        05  WS-FOOD         PIC 99.
```

The SEARCH can only be used with an indexed table. The identifier used with the search must be the data-name containing the OCCURS and INDEXED clause.

```
SEARCH WS-ZOO
```

not

```
SEARCH WS-CHART.
```

The condition is the same as any valid IF condition and the imperative statement is only executed when the condition is found.

```
SET WS-INDA TO 1.
SEARCH WS-ZOO
     WHEN WS-PET (WS-INDA) = "CAMEL"
     ADD WS-FOOD (WS-INDA) TO CAMEL-FOOD.
```

The index-name is SET to 1 so that the search starts at the first item of the table, it then proceeds sequentially through the table. The first test it makes is, THE END? – if the table has been completely searched and no CAMEL found then control passes to the statement following the search. The next test is, WS-PET (WS-INDA) = "CAMEL". If it is not, then the index-name is automatically set up by 1 and control automatically returns to the SEARCH. The index-name WS-INDA must be used to test the correct WS-PET. If it is a CAMEL then the ADD is executed and then control passes to the next sentence. The index-name will be left, referencing the occurrence with CAMEL in it, and the SEARCH stops.

If a CAMEL is not found you may want to execute a different piece of code:

```
SET WS-INDA TO 1.
SEARCH WS-ZOO
     AT END GO TO NO-CAMEL
     WHEN WS-PET (WS-INDA) = "CAMEL"
     ADD WS-FOOD (WS-INDA) TO CAMEL-FOOD.
```

If no camel is found control will pass to NO-CAMEL.

There may be more than one CAMEL in the list, so having found a CAMEL we want to return to the search.

```
        SET WS-INDA TO 1.
PARA-SEARCH.
        SEARCH WS-ZOO
             WHEN WS-PET (WS-INDA) = "CAMEL"
             ADD WS-FOOD (WS-INDA) TO CAMEL-FOOD
             SET WS-INDA UP BY 1
             GO TO PARA-SEARCH.
```

If a CAMEL is found its feed is added to the CAMEL FOOD total, the index-name is incremented by 1 and control passed back to the search. The index-name has to be explicitly incremented because the search only does it automatically if the condition is *not* met. Using this method the search will always end with the AT END clause, i.e. the table is exhausted.

Further procedure division exercises

Write the COBOL code for the following:

1 A field named WS–AREA should contain three A's before the hyphen. If it does not, pass control to ZZ–INVALID.

2 A field named WA–DESC contains a number of xs at the start of the field. Replace them with spaces.

3 Move the contents of BA–C to CA–AREA, followed by contents of BA–B up to but not including the *, followed by the contents of BA–A.

4 Separate the contents of DA–NAME into FA–A, FA–M, FA–B and FA–D. The delimiter separating these pieces of data is an =.

5 Search the following table for the seed PETUNIA. Having found it, add the number of packets to SEED–TOTAL. If PETUNIA is not found, pass control to NO–PETS.

```
01  WS-GARDEN.
    03  WS-FLOWERS OCCURS 100 INDEXED BY IND-SEED.
        05  WS-SEED      PIC X(10).
        05  WS-PKTS      PIC 9(4).
```

6 A data field WS–PARAM is to be accepted by the program and then displayed with the literal "MESSAGE".

7 Write a CALL statement to a module with the program-id CALCPAY written in COBOL.
   The parameters to be passed have the same data hyphen names in the main program and the module, CALCPAY.
   The procedure division statement in CALCPAY is:

```
PROCEDURE DIVISION USING WS-FIELD-IN
                         WS-FIELD-OUT.
```

8 Write a COPY statement for the following. In PARA–A copy the coding held in a file named PARACOPY.

13

Compiling, Testing, Documenting

Program preparation

Once the program has been coded, checked and dry run it is ready for data preparation. The coded or source program can be prepared for the computer on cards, paper tape, magnetic tape or magnetic disc, or it can be typed in directly using a video terminal. In this example cards are used for the source program.

Each line of coding will be punched on to a card: entries in Area A will start in column 8; entries in Area B will start from column 12 of the punched card. Mistakes might be made when punching the program, bad writing can also cause errors. The card can be interpreted, this is a printed version of the punched holes at the top of the card. This interpreting helps the programmer check the punching; it does not help the computer. When all the cards are punched and checked the program is ready for compilation.

Compilation

The COBOL compiler is a piece of software that reads program cards. It outputs a listing of those cards, followed by a list of errors that have been detected. The listing of the program has a number printed on each coded line; these line numbers are used by the compiler to pinpoint errors. Remember, the errors are *syntax* errors not logic errors.

Extracts from a program with syntax errors:

```
41      WORKING-STORAGE SECTION.
42      01  WS-TOT              PIC 9(20).
43      01  WS-A                PIC X(10).
44          03  WS-B            PIC 99
```

```
45              03 WS-C           XX.
LINE 42         Numeric picture greater than 18.
LINE 43         Group field has picture clause.
LINE 44         No fullstop.
LINE 45         PICture clause missing.
73      PROCEDURE DIVISION.
74              OPEN IN-FILE.
75              MOVE WS-DATA TO 10.
76      BB-READ
77              READ IN-FILE AT END.
78              GO TO ZZ-END.
LINE 74         No paragraph name after PROCEDURE DIVISION.
LINE 74         No opening mode ie: I-O, INPUT, OUTPUT.
LINE 75         MOVE TO Literal is not allowed.
LINE 76         No fullstop.
LINE 77         No imperative statement after AT END.
LINE 78         Undeclared paragraph, ZZ-END.
```

These are the syntax errors that can be found by the compiler.

When the compilation listing is returned to you, you must carefully work through the error messages, deciding what is wrong with your program code. You must decide how to correct all the errors and write the correct lines down.

If you have coded your program carefully you may have very few syntax errors. The errors can be corrected using a piece of software called an *editor*.

The program cards are stored on a magnetic file and each program line has a number. The editor can correct the program lines by referencing the lines that are in error and substituting the correct piece of code. This can be done using card input or by entering the corrections through a VDU. The latter method is widely used for this phase of program development.

Having corrected your source program, you compile it again. The program should now be error-free or *clean*. It may take a number of edits and compiles to clean compile a large program.

When the program is clean compiled the second function of the compiler takes place. Each line of coding is broken down into machine code instructions, and those instructions are stored on a magnetic file which is called the *object* program.

Testing

Having stored the object program, testing can commence. To test a program you must design and create test data. There are pieces of software available to help you create data. For simple sequential files it is easy to create the records from punched cards.

Test data must be designed to cater for every combination of data field, it must test every path in your program. For an update program two files must be created and care must be taken to make sure key fields on the two files correlate.

For a print program there must be a large enough volume of data to test page throw and page numbering routines.

For a validation program all field errors must be catered for, as well as a good number of correct records.

Having created and listed the test data you should prepare the *expected results*. Each record to be output from the program, both on a printed report and on magnetic files, should be documented. The expected results will speed up the testing process of your program. You then submit your program for testing. Your object program will be loaded into the computer's store and execution will begin. The program will open and read the test data files and will output data files. During the testing of a program the program may halt with a serious logic error, e.g.:

- reading a file without opening it;
- falling through the end of program logic;
- looping around the same code continually;
- dividing by zero.

If this happens you will correct the error, recompile the program and test it again. More likely, your program will finish when the stop run is executed. A listing of any output files should be obtained in order for you to check them against the expected results.

Compilation, creation of test data and program testing can be initiated through a VDU. This method of testing a program 'interactively' can improve the programmer's productivity by speeding up the program development process.

Debugging

By checking the program-produced output against the expected results you can easily determine what your program is doing wrong. If it is printing a total wrongly there will be an error in the totalling part of your program or you may be printing it incorrectly. This process of finding the logic errors in your program is called *debugging*. (This expression comes from a problem with a computer when an insect was found to be the cause. Hence debugging, or getting the bugs out.)

Having found the program errors and corrected them, you will recompile and retest the program. By repeating the process you will eventually have a working program. You can prove this by having program output results the same as the expected results.

You may need more than one set of test data to fully test a program.

Documentation

The working program is now ready for suite and system testing. This is often done by someone else and you should hand your program over with its associated documentation. Documentation is a commonly ignored aspect of a programmer's work but it is very important. A program can have a life of twenty years, running every week or day. It is unlikely that you will be available for twenty years to maintain it, enhance it, or correct it. You must document it so that someone else can do those things.

The minimum documentation should be:

- the program specification;
- amendments to the specification;
- up to date flowchart;
- program source listing;
- test data listings;
- expected results;
- actual results.

Final testing and production

A program will first be suite tested. This is done with small test data files. This test checks that programs interface correctly, and that the file output from one program can be read and processed correctly by the next program.

The next stage is *system testing*. This is usually done using *live* data prepared by the input clerks. This test tries to simulate the production environment. Errors can often occur in programs when large volumes are processed – total fields may be too small, or an unusual case may be found which has not been catered for. This might result in changes being made to program specifications and program coding. If this is the case, recompilation and testing would have to take place.

When the system test has worked successfully and the user is happy with the results then the program is ready for production running.

14

Example Program

This chapter contains a full program specification with its associated documentation.

(a) The specification.
(b) The program flowchart.
(c) The compilation listing.
(d) The test data.
(e) The program results.

The specification is a detailed document which you should now understand well enough to follow the rest of the documentation. Program specifications are presented in various forms and to varying standards. There is the tale of the program specification written on the back of a cigarette packet. You must insist that you have a specification that clearly defines what is required. File layouts are presented in different ways, sometimes on preprinted forms. However they are written, they must specify each field for size, usage and a reasonable description of what that field will contain.

The flowchart is an accurate diagram of what the program procedure division does. You may produce a slightly different solution, but that does not matter. What matters is that the flowchart has been dry run and produces correct results.

The compilation listing is of the final working program. There will have been many incorrect listings produced during the development of the program, some with syntax errors, some with logic errors. Only the working program listing will form part of the final documentation. The printed listing is easier to read than your original written code. Notice the numbers printed at the left side of the coded line, this is the number used for syntax error messages.

The test data must be carefully designed; the input sequential file must contain enough data to test the various page throws. There is data for three shops: the first shop has ten detail records, and part fills a page. The second shop has thirty detail records and fills one page and part of another, and the third shop has twenty-five detail records and fills one page completely. The detail records contain various type and quantity values and varying numbers of type and quantity. They also contain some supplier codes that are not on the supplier name file and, therefore, test that NO NAME ON FILE is printed correctly. There is an example of the coded and the printed test data. There is a computer-produced list of the DA01 file and a hand written example of the DA02 file. The expected results are not shown here, but the expected total quantities and the report output were produced.

Finally the results are produced by the computer. They must be meticulously checked before you declare your program correct and working.

This forms your complete final documentation.

A Program specification

1 *Identification*
Program identifier   SHOP.

2 *Introduction*
The purpose of this program is to print a stock analysis for each shop. A shop has many records, each with details of a part and a supplier, each part can have up to four sub-codes with associated quantities of stock. The report starts a new page for each shop, the detail line includes the supplier name taken from a supplier indexed sequential file. The detail quantities are accumulated and printed at the end of each shop.

3 *Characteristics*
Programming language   COBOL
Files used   1 sequential input
                                               1 sequential output
                                               1 indexed sequential

4 *Processing tasks*
   (a) To create an output report for each shop code.
   (b) To print headings at the top of each page maintaining a page count.
   (c) To print a detail line for each input record.

(d) To accumulate the detail quantities and print a total at the end of each shop.

5 *Data*

(a) The input shop stock file contains 60 character long records. There is only one type of record. The file is sorted into shop code order and part code within shop code. See 8(a) for details.

(b) The supplier detail file contains records 76 characters long. There is only one type of record. The file is indexed on the supply code field. See 8(b) for details.

(c) A parameter card containing a date DDMMYY.

6 *Results*

The report file has 132 character long records. See print layout. There are four heading lines:

- Line 1 contains a page number which must be incremented for every page and zero suppressed when printed. A date which is accepted at the start of the program.
- Line 2 contains asterisks to highlight the heading line.
- Line 3 contains fixed heading details.
- Line 4 contains fixed heading details.

There are three detail lines.

- Line 6 contains the shop code and name of the shop stock being processed, this line will appear at the top of every page including continuation pages.
- Line 16 contains the total quantity value for that shop, this line will appear at the end of each shop.

A maximum of twenty-five detail lines can be printed on a page. Each detail line is double spaced. The total detail (see line 16) may appear on line 58 if the page is full.

7 *Processing*

(a) Accept the parameter card containing the accounting date and store it for printing. Print the four heading lines.

(b) Read the shop stock file,

(i) if the end of file has been reached

- print the final shop total
- display the message END OF PROGRAM SHOP
- close the files
- stop the program

140   *Computer Programming in COBOL*

(ii) if the shop code has changed

- print the shop total
- zeroise the quantity total
- print new headings
- print new shop code and name

(iii) if the line count indicates a full page

- print new headings
- print shop code and name.

(c) Create the detail line from the shop stock record. Use the supply-code to read the supply file.

- If the record is not on the supply file print NO NAME ON FILE, instead of the name.
- If the record is on the supply file print the supply name field.
- Accumulate the four quantity fields into the shop quantity field.

8 *File layouts*

(a) Input stock detail file – DA01 – a disc file.
Sequential file, sorted in shop code, part code sequence.

Shop code	3 numeric digits
Shop name	20 alphanumeric characters
Part code	5 numeric digits
Supplier's code	6 alphanumeric characters
Area check code	2 alphanumeric characters

The following group of two fields occurs 4 times.

Type	2 alphanumeric characters
Quantity	4 numeric digits

(b) Input supplier detail file – DA02 – a disc file.
Indexed sequential, key field supplier code.

Supplier code	6 alphanumeric characters
Supplier name	25 alphanumeric characters
Supplier address	40 alphanumeric characters
Supplier area	5 alphanumeric characters

(c) Output stock analysis report – LP03 – a line printer file.
The layout is opposite.

LPO3 layout

A print layout chart showing column headings and data field formats:

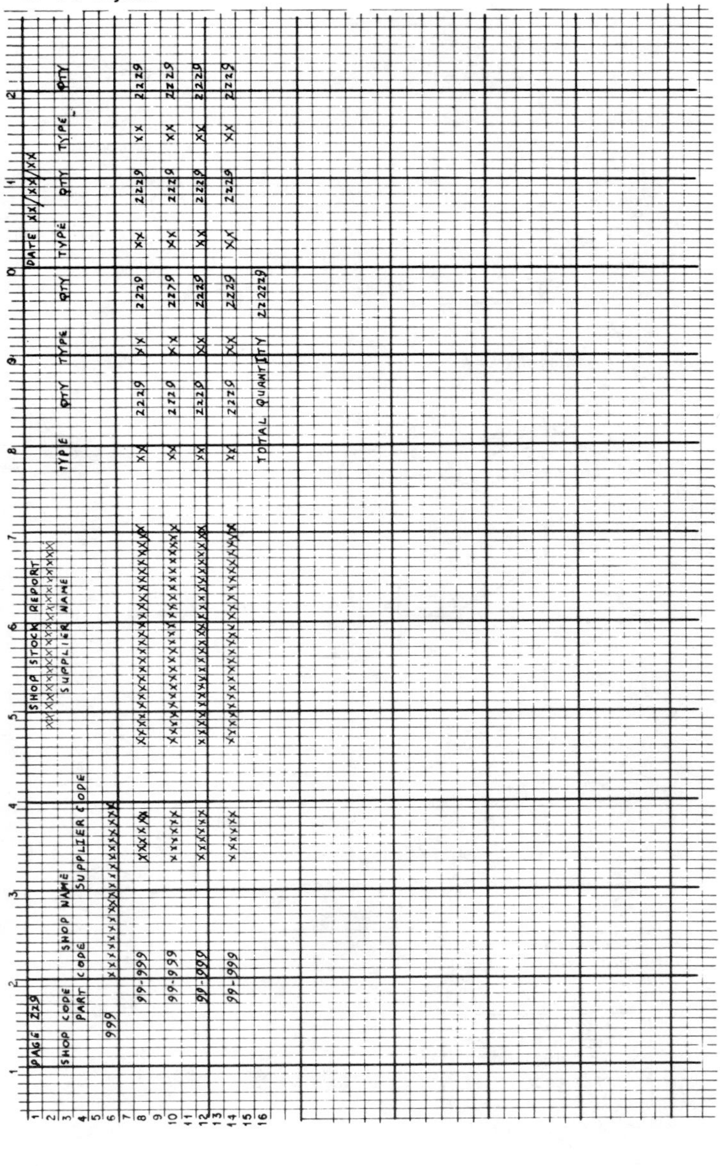

Position	Field	Format
1	PAGE	ZZ9
2	SHOP CODE	
	PART CODE	999
3	SHOP NAME	XXXXXXXXXXX
	SUPPLIER CODE	XXXXXXX
4	SUPPLIER CODE	
5	SHOP STOCK REPORT	XXXXXXXXX
	SUPPLIER NAME	XXXXXXXXXX
8	TYPE	XX
	QTY	ZZZ9
9	TYPE	XX
	QTY	ZZZ9
	TOTAL QUANTITY	ZZ ZZZ9
11	DATE	XX/XX/XX
	TYPE	XX
	QTY	ZZZ9
21	TYPE	XX
	QTY	ZZZ9

Line	PART CODE	SUPPLIER CODE	TYPE	QTY	TYPE	QTY	TYPE	QTY	TYPE	QTY
8	999	XXXX XX	XX	ZZZ9	XX	ZZZ9	XX	ZZZ9	XX	ZZZ9
10	99 999	XX XX XX	XX	ZZZ9	XX	ZZZ9	XX	ZZZ9	XX	ZZZ9
12	99 999	XX XX XX	XX	ZZZ9	XX	ZZZ9	XX	ZZZ9	XX	ZZZ9
14	99 999	XX XX XX	XX	ZZZ9	XX	ZZZ9	XX	ZZZ9	XX	ZZZ9

B   Program flowchart   SHOP

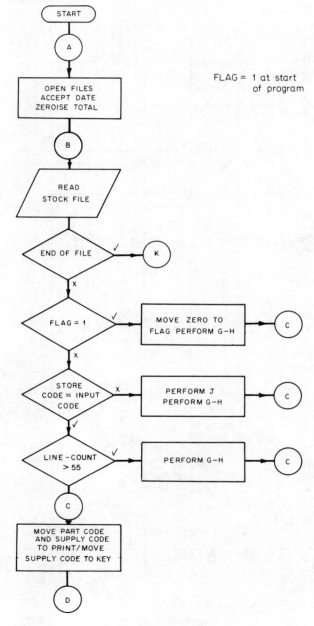

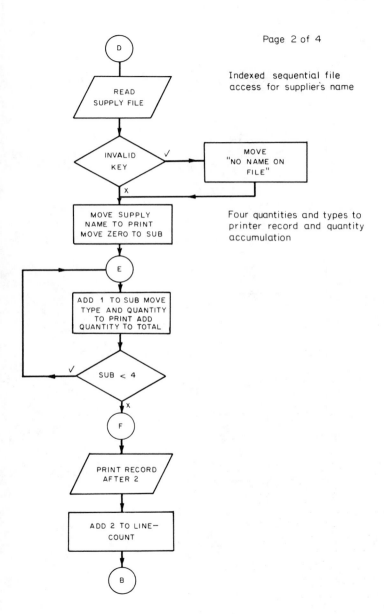

Indexed sequential file access for supplier's name

Four quantities and types to printer record and quantity accumulation

144 Computer Programming in COBOL

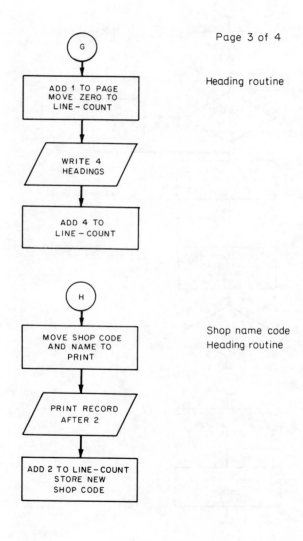

Heading routine

Shop name code
Heading routine

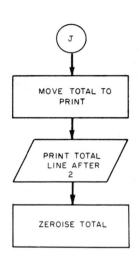

Total line routine

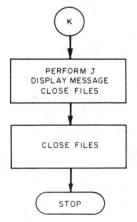

Final routine
Print last total

146   *Computer Programming in COBOL*

C Compilation listing

```
                              COBOL        COMPILATION 1981/03/06 01:13:19

                        S O U R C E   L I S T I N G

1        IDENTIFICATION DIVISION.
2        PROGRAM-ID. SHOP.
3    *
4    *        THIS PROGRAM PRINTS A STOCK ANALYSIS FOR EACH SHOP
5    *
6        ENVIRONMENT DIVISION.
7        CONFIGURATION SECTION.
8        SOURCE-COMPUTER.
9            ICL-2972.
10       OBJECT-COMPUTER.
11           ICL-2972.
12       INPUT-OUTPUT SECTION.
13       FILE-CONTROL.
14           SELECT IN-STOCK      ASSIGN TO DA01.
15           SELECT OUT-REPORT    ASSIGN TO LP03.
16           SELECT IN-SUPPLY     ASSIGN TO DA02
17               ORGANISATION INDEXED
18               ACCESS RANDOM
19               RECORD KEY IS IN-SUPPLY-CODE.
20       DATA DIVISION.
21       FILE SECTION.
22       FD  IN-STOCK.
23       01  IN-STOCK-REC.
24           03 IN-SHOP-CODE      PIC 999.
25           03 IN-SHOP-NAME      PIC X(20).
26           03 IN-PART-CODE      PIC 9(5).
```

```
27        03 IN-SUPP-CODE        PIC X(6).
28        03 FILLER              PIC XX.
29        03 IN-GROUP OCCURS 4 TIMES.
30           05 IN-TYPE          PIC XX.
31           05 IN-QNTY          PIC 9(4).
32    *
33    *     SHOP STOCK DETAILS WITH 4 SUB TYPES FOR EACH PART CODE
34    *
35    FD IN-SUPPLY.
36    01 IN-SUPPLY-REC.
37        03 IN-SUPPLY-CODE      PIC X(6).
38        03 IN-SUPPLY-NAME      PIC X(25).
39        03 FILLER              PIC X(45).
40    *
41    *     INDEXED SEQUENTIAL FILE INDEXED ON SUPPLY CODE
42    *
43    FD OUT-REPORT.
44    01 REP-REC.
45        03 FILLER              PIC X(17).
46        03 REP-PART            PIC 991-999.
47        03 FILLER              PIC X(10).
48        03 REP-SUPP-CODE       PIC X(6).
49        03 FILLER              PIC X(7).
50        03 REP-SUPP-NAME       PIC X(25).
51        03 FILLER              PIC X(7).
52        03 REP-GROUP OCCURS 4 TIMES.
53           05 REP-TYP          PIC XX.
54           05 FILLER           PIC X(3).
55           05 REP-QNTY         PIC ZZ9.
56           05 FILLER           PIC X(3).
```

```
                            COBOL                    COMPILATION 1981/03/06 01:13:19

                        S O U R C E   L I S T I N G

  57            03 FILLER              PIC X(6).
  58      *
  59      *  PRINT RECORD - TYPE AND QUANTITY ARE REPEATED 4 TIMES
  60      *                 ON ONE LINE
  61   01 REP-REC-HD.
  62            03 FILLER              PIC X(13).
  63            03 REP-SHOP-CODE       PIC 999.
  64            03 FILLER              PIC X(4).
  65            03 REP-SHOP-NAME       PIC X(20).
  66            03 FILLER              PIC X(92).
  67      *
  68      *  SECOND PRINT RECORD TYPE - SHOP CODE AND NAME
  69      *
  70   WORKING-STORAGE SECTION.
  71   01 WS-DATE          PIC X(6).
  72   01 WS-HEAD-1.
  73            03 FILLER              PIC X(15) VALUE "        PAGE".
  74            03 WS-PAGE             PIC ZZ9.
  75            03 FILLER              PIC X(32) VALUE SPACES.
  76            03 FILLER              PIC X(50) VALUE "SHOP STOCK REPORT".
  77            03 FILLER              PIC X(5)  VALUE "DATE".
  78            03 WS-IN-DATE          PIC XX/XX/XX.
  79      *
  80      *  THE HEADING LINE IS BROKEN DOWN TO AID EASIER DESCRIPTION
  81      *  FILLER IS USED WHENEVER A DATA-NAME
  82      *                 IS NOT REQUIRED
```

```
83   *
84   01  WS-HEAD-2.
85       03  FILLER          PIC X(48) VALUE SPACES.
86       03  FILLER          PIC X(21) VALUE ALL "***********************".
87   01  WS-HEAD-3           PIC X(32) VALUE
88       "    SHOP CODE      SHOP NAME".
89   01  WS-HEAD-4.
90       03  FILLER                    PIC X(15) VALUE SPACES.
91       03  FILLER                    PIC X(108) VALUE
92       "PART CODE      SUPPLIER CODE      SUPPLIER NAME
93   -   "   TYPE    QTY    TYPE    QTY    TYPE    QTY    TYPE    QTY".
94   01  WS-SUB               PIC 9 COMP SYNC RIGHT.
95   01  WS-PAGE-COUNT        PIC 999 COMP SYNC RIGHT.
96   01  WS-LINE-COUNT        PIC 99 COMP SYNC RIGHT.
97   01  WS-STORE-SHOP-CODE   PIC 999.
98   01  WS-TOTAL-QUANTITY    PIC 9(6) COMP SYNC RIGHT.
99   01  WS-FLAG             PIC X VALUE "1".
100  01  WS-QNTY-LINE.
101      03  FILLER          PIC X(78) VALUE SPACES.
102      03  FILLER          PIC X(16) VALUE "TOTAL QUANTITY".
103      03  WS-QNTY         PIC Z(5)9.
104  PROCEDURE DIVISION.
105  AA-START.
106      OPEN INPUT IN-STOCK.
107      OPEN I-O IN-SUPPLY.
108      OPEN OUTPUT OUT-REPORT.
109      ACCEPT WS-DATE.
110      MOVE WS-DATE TO WS-IN-DATE.
111      INITIALISE WS-TOTAL-QUANTITY.
112  BB-READ.
```

```
                        COBOL         COMPILATION 1981/03/06 01:13:19

                    S O U R C E   L I S T I N G


113  *
114         READ IN-STOCK AT END GO TO KK-END.
115         IF WS-FLAG = "1"
116             MOVE ZERO TO WS-FLAG
117             PERFORM GG-HEADINGS THRU HH-SHOP-HEAD
118             GO TO CC-LINE.
119  *
120  *   WS-FLAG IS A FIRST TIME FLAG, IT TRIGGERS FIRST PAGE HEADINGS
121  *
122         IF IN-SHOP-CODE NOT = WS-STORE-SHOP-CODE
123             PERFORM JJ-TOTAL
124             PERFORM GG-HEADINGS THRU HH-SHOP-HEAD
125             GO TO CC-LINE.
126  *
127  *   ON CHANGE OF SHOP CODE TOTALS ARE PRINTED AND A NEW
128  *       PAGE STARTED
129         IF WS-LINE-COUNT > 55
130             PERFORM GG-HEADINGS THRU HH-SHOP-HEAD.
131  *
132  *   LINE COUNT INDICATES FULL PAGE, PRINT NEW HEADINGS
133  *
134     CC-LINE.
135         MOVE SPACES TO REP-REC.
136         MOVE IN-PART-CODE TO REP-PART.
137         MOVE IN-SUPP-CODE TO REP-SUPP-CODE.
138  *
```

```
139    *    MOVE THE TWO FIELDS TO THE PRINT RECORD
140    *
141    DD-READ-SUPPLY.
142        MOVE IN-SUPP-CODE TO IN-SUPPLY-CODE.
143        READ IN-SUPPLY INVALID KEY
144            MOVE "NO NAME ON FILE" TO IN-SUPPLY-NAME.
145    *
146    *    READ SUPPLY FILE, IF NOT ON FILE USE STANDARD MESSAGE
147    *
148        MOVE IN-SUPPLY-NAME TO REP-SUPP-NAME.
149        MOVE ZERO TO WS-SUB.
150    EE-LOOP.
151        ADD 1 TO WS-SUB.
152        MOVE IN-TYPE (WS-SUB) TO REP-TYP (WS-SUB).
153        MOVE IN-QNTY (WS-SUB) TO REP-QNTY (WS-SUB).
154        ADD IN-QNTY (WS-SUB) TO WS-TOTAL-QUANTITY.
155        IF WS-SUB < 4 GO TO EE-LOOP.
156    *
157    *    MOVE FOUR TYPES AND QUANTITIES, ACCUMULATE QUANTITIES
158    *
159    FF-REP-PRINT.
160        WRITE REP-REC AFTER 2.
161        ADD 2 TO WS-LINE-COUNT.
162        GO TO BB-READ.
163    *
164    *    PRINT DETAIL LINE, INCREMENT LINE COUNT, READ
165    *
166    GG-HEADINGS.
167        ADD 1 TO WS-PAGE-COUNT.
168        MOVE WS-PAGE-COUNT TO WS-PAGE.
```

```
COMPILATION 1981/03/06 01:13:19

COBOL

SOURCE LISTING

169        MOVE ZERO TO WS-LINE-COUNT.
170        WRITE REP-REC FROM WS-HEAD-1 AFTER PAGE.
171        WRITE REP-REC FROM WS-HEAD-2 AFTER 1.
172        WRITE REP-REC FROM WS-HEAD-3 AFTER 1.
173        WRITE REP-REC FROM WS-HEAD-4 AFTER 1.
174        ADD 4 TO WS-LINE-COUNT.
175    *
176    *  INCREMENT PAGE COUNT, PRINT HEADINGS, INCREMENT LINE COUNT
177    *
178    HH-SHOP-HEAD.
179        MOVE SPACES TO REP-REC-HD.
180        MOVE IN-SHOP-CODE TO REP-SHOP-CODE.
181        MOVE IN-SHOP-NAME TO REP-SHOP-NAME.
182        WRITE REP-REC-HD AFTER 2.
183        ADD 2 TO WS-LINE-COUNT.
184        MOVE IN-SHOP-CODE TO WS-STORE-SHOP-CODE.
185    *
186    *  PRINT SHOP CODE AND NAME, STORE SHOP CODE
187    *
188    JJ-TOTAL.
189        MOVE WS-TOTAL-QUANTITY TO WS-QNTY.
190        WRITE REP-REC FROM WS-QNTY-LINE AFTER 2.
191        INITIALISE WS-TOTAL-QUANTITY.
192    *
193    *  PRINT TOTAL LINE, SET TOTAL TO ZERO
194    *
```

```
       195
       196
       197
       198
       199
       200
       201

KK-END.
       PERFORM JJ-TOTAL.
       MOVE SPACES TO REP-REC.
       WRITE REP-REC AFTER PAGE.
       DISPLAY "END OF PROGRAM SHOP".
       CLOSE IN-STOCK IN-SUPPLY OUT-REPORT.
       STOP RUN.

195
196
197
198
199
200
201
```

D The test data computer listing of DA01 test file

```
103SHOP   IN  TOWN   01347206511AA010010070012091002102000
103SHOP   IN  TOWN   02134800101AB0313500040712050012060000
103SHOP   IN  TOWN   11977521774AC07000009072111083799147 7
103SHOP   IN  TOWN   13446410664BB0119760312040400 02
103SHOP   IN  TOWN   15677800101BI051111AA1104
103SHOP   IN  TOWN   15678994126TB0492000960201230461700 21
103SHOP   IN  TOWN   20401719224TK0611471100921301031501 44
103SHOP   IN  TOWN   23447206511WV09001299000 27AB0011BT0022
103SHOP   IN  TOWN   27766994126WX0300300700040081000092110
103SHOP   IN  TOWN   30987410664YZ110060
377SHOP   ON  THE  HILL   11977521774AB120000 22000032217 74 23046
377SHOP   ON  THE  HILL   13846224660AC24900329405 0346666
377SHOP   ON  THE  HILL   15678994126AD032116112183133004
377SHOP   ON  THE  HILL   23447206511BZ05009706009807010 00081000
377SHOP   ON  THE  HILL   30987410664DB0611111312302300 46530007
377SHOP   ON  THE  HILL   37191795520DK1401063601704801306 00114
377SHOP   ON  THE  HILL   39227719224DL250003
377SHOP   ON  THE  HILL   41667203384MT970006
377SHOP   ON  THE  HILL   41701795520MP9200009312449412029 51307
377SHOP   ON  THE  HILL   46235521774LV1100115100126 10017
377SHOP   ON  THE  HILL   48996416203TW301003401006500021
377SHOP   ON  THE  HILL   50100634821KZ3A11233247664K2036 4Z9111
377SHOP   ON  THE  HILL   56304412603ZBAZ0020BX0035BY0222
377SHOP   ON  THE  HILL   56306203384AC21001022001222 30013
377SHOP   ON  THE  HILL   58844521774CD3110003223332 23000
377SHOP   ON  THE  HILL   61127410664YU100014
377SHOP   ON  THE  HILL   80442390211PA990091
377SHOP   ON  THE  HILL   88891800101XX170130
377SHOP   ON  THE  HILL   88903994126T5607229A045692 1977AB1978
377SHOP   ON  THE  HILL   89200766443MX120017130060
377SHOP   ON  THE  HILL   89307525110LZ440052550039
```

```
377SHOP ON THE HILL   89311927321KX910177920188
377SHOP ON THE HILL   89416206511BI14017717011180230
377SHOP ON THE HILL   90111206511TU160100200144260176302011
377SHOP ON THE HILL   90112203176PM500366
377SHOP ON THE HILL   95522412603DP771900880144990177
377SHOP ON THE HILL   96623766443BA000040
377SHOP ON THE HILL   96677994126KL2A10002B3000B31000
377SHOP ON THE HILL   97717525110SI42001043O010
377SHOP ON THE HILL   98800412603TW770050790500
554SHOP IN THE VALE   01347206511AA010010070012091002102000
554SHOP IN THE VALE   03447711111TT0400101201001131000
554SHOP IN THE VALE   11977521774XX031222
554SHOP IN THE VALE   15678994126YY011777
554SHOP IN THE VALE   27766994126A10414416122
554SHOP IN THE VALE   30987410664DB061111113123023004653007
554SHOP IN THE VALE   41701795520MP920000931244941202951307
554SHOP IN THE VALE   48996416203TW301003
554SHOP IN THE VALE   49977927321BBAA0000
554SHOP IN THE VALE   50100634821BZ3A1123300100
554SHOP IN THE VALE   56306203384AC210100
554SHOP IN THE VALE   61127410664YM200010
554SHOP IN THE VALE   74193766443   901111
554SHOP IN THE VALE   88891800101XX10947612300 0
554SHOP IN THE VALE   89200766443MP120700
554SHOP IN THE VALE   89311927321   170010270110
554SHOP IN THE VALE   89312927321   400002050040
554SHOP IN THE VALE   89416206511BI140150
554SHOP IN THE VALE   90111206511TM14001015002020000773400 99
554SHOP IN THE VALE   90112203176PM500050
554SHOP IN THE VALE   96677994126BL2A00772B0999
554SHOP IN THE VALE   97717525110BA
554SHOP IN THE VALE   97724412603    100070
554SHOP IN THE VALE   98800412603TW400066500077
554SHOP IN THE VALE   99946203176MF200093
```

Sequence No.	7 8	Data	Identification (73–75)
203117	6	SMITH AND BRØWN BØURNEMØUTH	S1723
203384	6	JØHN GREEN LTD BASINGSTØKE	S2144
206511	1	BRØWN LTD MAIDSTØNE	SE721
410664	8	BLACK AND BLUE LTD IPSWICH	E4433
412603	6	GEØRGE AND SØNS NEWCASTLE	NE216
521774	M	CTAVISH LTD EPINBURGH	SC489
525110	0	CAMPBELL AND SØNS GLASGØW	SC910
719224	8	ØRDER, PARTS, LTD CARLISLE	N3476
766443	7	TAYLØR, BRØS. MANCHESTER	NE266
795220	0	CARTER LTD LIVERPØØL	NE311
800010	1	JØNES AND SØNS CARDIFF	W1212
927321	6	GREY LTP BRISTØL	W4277
994126	0	DEVLIN SUPPLY LTD PLYMØUTH	SW984

Test data for file DAO2
written on coding sheets
ready for data preparation

E Program results

Note that these program results are intended to indicate content only; limitations of space do not permit display showing actual spacing and layout.

```
                    SHOP STOCK REPORT                        DATE 19/02/81
               ****************************
```

PART CODE	SUPPLIER CODE	SUPPLIER NAME	TYPE	QTY	TYPE	QTY	TYPE	QTY	TYPE	QTY
SHOP CODE	SHOP NAME									
103	SHOP IN TOWN									
01-347	206511	BROWN LTD	01	10	07	12	09	1002	10	2000
02-134	800101	JONES AND SONS	03	1300	04	712	05	12	06	0
11-977	521774	MCTAVISH LTD	07	0	09	721	11	837	99	1477
13-446	410664	BLACK AND BLUE LTD	01	1976	03	1204	04	2		0
15-677	800101	JONES AND SONS	05	1111	AA	1104		0		0
15-678	994126	DEVON SUPPLY LTD	04	9200	09	6020	12	3046	17	21
20-401	719224	BORDER PARTS LTD	06	1147	11	92	13	103	15	144
23-447	206511	BROWN LTD	09	12	99	27	A3	11	BT	22
27-766	994126	DEVON SUPPLY LTD	03	30	07	40	08	1000	09	2110
30-987	410664	BLACK AND BLUE LTD	11	60		0		0		0

```
                              TOTAL QUANTITY      36565
```

SHOP STOCK REPORT
****

DATE 19/02/81

SHOP CODE   SHOP NAME

377   SHOP ON THE HILL

PART CODE	SUPPLIER CODE	SUPPLIER NAME	TYPE	QTY	TYPE	QTY	TYPE	QTY	TYPE	QTY
11-977	521774	MCTAVISH LTD	12	0	22	0	32	2177	42	3046
13-846	224660	NO NAME ON FILE	24	9003	29	4050	34	666		0
15-678	994126	DEVON SUPPLY LTD	03	2116	11	2183	13	3004		0
23-447	206511	BROWN LTD	05	97	06	98	07	100	08	1000
30-987	410664	BLACK AND BLUE LTD	06	1111	13	1230	23	46	53	7
37-191	795520	CARTER LTD	14	106	36	170	48	130	60	114
39-227	719224	BORDER PARTS LTD	25	3		0		0		0
41-667	203384	JOHN GREEN LTD	97	6		0		0		0
41-701	795520	CARTER LTD	92	0	93	1244	94	1202	95	1307
46-233	521774	MCTAVISH LTD	11	11	51	12	61	17		0
48-996	416203	NO NAME ON FILE	30	1003	40	1006	50	21		0
50-100	634821	NO NAME ON FILE	3A	1123	32	4766	4K	2036	4Z	9111
56-304	412603	GEORGE AND SONS	AZ	20	3X	35	BY	222		0
56-306	203384	JOHN GREEN LTD	21	10	22	12	22	3001	3	0
58-844	521774	MCTAVISH LTD	31	1000	32	2333	22	3000		0
61-127	410664	BLACK AND BLUE LTD	10	14		0		0		0
80-442	390211	NO NAME ON FILE	99	91		0		0		0
88-891	800101	JONES AND SONS	17	130		0		0		0
88-903	994126	DEVON SUPPLY LTD	56	722	9A	456	9Z	1977	AB	1978
89-200	766443	TAYLOR BROS	12	17	13	60		0		0
89-307	525110	CAMPBELL AND SONS	44	52	55	39		0		0
89-311	927321	GREY LTD	91	177	92	188		0		0
89-416	206511	BROWN LTD	14	177	17	111	18	230		0
90-111	206511	BROWN LTD	16	100	20	144	26	176	30	2011
90-112	203176	SMITH AND BROWN	50	366		0		0		0

SHOP STOCK REPORT
****

DATE 19/02/81

SHOP CODE PART CODE	SHOP NAME SUPPLIER CODE	SUPPLIER NAME	TYPE	QTY	TYPE	QTY	TYPE	QTY	TYPE	QTY
95-522	412603	GEORGE AND SONS	77	1900	88	144	99	177		0
96-623	766443	TAYLOR BROS	00	40		0		0		0
96-677	994126	DEVON SUPPLY LTD	2A	1000	2B	3000	B3	1000		0
97-717	525110	CAMPBELL AND SONS	42	10	43	10		0		0
98-800	412603	GEORGE AND SONS	77	50	79	500		0		0

TOTAL QUANTITY 86002

PAGE   4

SHOP STOCK REPORT
****

DATE   19/02/81

SHOP CODE   SHOP NAME

554   SHOP IN THE VALE

PART CODE	SUPPLIER CODE	SUPPLIER NAME	TYPE	QTY	TYPE	QTY	TYPE	QTY	TYPE	QTY
01-347	206511	BROWN LTD	01	10	07	12	09	1002	10	2000
03-447	711111	NO NAME ON FILE	TO	4001	01	2010	01	3100	0	0
11-977	521774	MCTAVISH LTD	03	1222		0		0		0
15-678	994126	DEVON SUPPLY LTD	01	1777		0		0		0
27-766	994126	DEVON SUPPLY LTD	10	4144	16	1222	23	46	53	0
30-987	410664	BLACK AND BLUE LTD	06	1111	13	1230	94	1202	95	7
41-701	795520	CARTER LTD	92	0	93	1244		0		1307
48-996	416203	NO NAME ON FILE	30	1003		0		0		0
49-977	927321	GREY LTD	AA	0		0		0		0
50-100	634821	NO NAME ON FILE	3A	1123	30	100		0		0
56-306	203384	JOHN GREEN LTD	21	100		0		0		0
61-127	410664	BLACK AND BLUE LTD	20	10		0		0		0
74-193	766443	TAYLOR BROS	90	1111		0		0		0
88-891	800101	JONES AND SONS	10	9476	12	3000		0		0
89-200	766443	TAYLOR BROS	12	700		0		0		0
89-311	927321	GREY LTD	17	10	27	110		0		0
89-312	927321	GREY LTD	40	2	05	40		0		0
89-416	206511	BROWN LTD	14	150		0		0		0
90-111	206511	BROWN LTD	14	10	15	20		0		0
90-112	203176	SMITH AND BROWN	50	50		0		0	34	99
96-677	994126	DEVON SUPPLY LTD	2A	77	2B	999		0		0
97-717	525110	CAMPBELL AND SONS		0		0		0		0
97-724	412603	GEORGE AND SONS	10	70		0		0		0
98-800	412603	GEORGE AND SONS	40	66	50	77		0		0
99-946	203176	SMITH AND BROWN	20	93		0		0		0

TOTAL QUANTITY 45220

15

Applications

Commercial business is the largest user of computer systems. Computers can now cope with the routine commercial work that is essential for a company's success with payroll systems probably the most common – even firms without computers buy computer bureaux services to produce their payroll. With developments in the banking clearing systems staff are paid without cash changing hands; this obviously gives better security.

Stock control systems are also important. As stores get larger, controlling stock becomes less feasible unless a computer system is developed. Companies cannot afford to overstock, and a control system can ensure that they do not.

Invoicing systems are also widely used – most household bills and credit card systems are invoiced by computer. This quick and accurate method of billing customers helps the company's cash flow and can improve its profitability. More recently there has been a trend in developing Management Information Systems. Now that the routine tasks are undertaken by computers there is more time and information to help management in decision-making. This information is usually captured by the stock control, payroll and invoicing systems and is presented in a different form for management. Production figures, cash flow, profitability, market trends and the cost of labour can all be collated and presented in reports.

Batch

Most of these applications are batch systems and can be run daily, weekly, monthly or annually, whatever cycle suits the system.

Let us look at a payroll system in more detail. Consider a system for a small factory of weekly paid staff who are paid in cash on Friday morning of each week. The pay week runs from Thursday morning to Wednesday evening. Fig. 13a is a systems diagram.

Program 1 – Validate
Each employee has a unique works number. Every day the foreman collects hours worked by each man including absence and overtime. On Thursday morning the foreman presents all this data to the payroll clerk. A pay detail form is completed with the works number, how many normal hours were worked and how many overtime hours. There will be one form per employee. These forms are sent for data preparation, one punched card for each form is produced. When all the data is prepared it is batched and sent to the computer for processing. The validate program checks the pay details for correct ranges of values and writes valid records to a magnetic tape file, any invalid records are printed on the rejection report. A record with details of 170 normal hours worked would clearly be invalid. These rejected records would be printed and the worker paid a normal week; adjustments would be made the following week.

Program 2 – Sort
The valid pay file is sorted, using a piece of sorting software, into works number sequence.

Program 3 – Pay calculation
This program is an update, it updates the *paymaster file* with details of this week's pay.

The *input paymaster file* is the same format as the *output paymaster*. This file is updated twice a week, once by the *pay calculation program* and once by the *master update program* run every Wednesday. (See Fig. 13b.) The amendments are used to delete a master record if someone leaves, add a new record if someone joins, and change details of a master record, e.g. new address, new married name, or new hourly rate. The update is run on Wednesday so that the pay suite has up-to-date master details. The pay calculation program matches the *sorted pay file* with the paymaster and, using hours worked details and master information, calculates the week's pay. These details are written to the current week's pay file for later printing. The *exception report* prints details of unmatched records, these can be paid manually if necessary.

Program 4 – Pay Print and Analysis
This program produces two reports. The first report, *pay detail*, prints

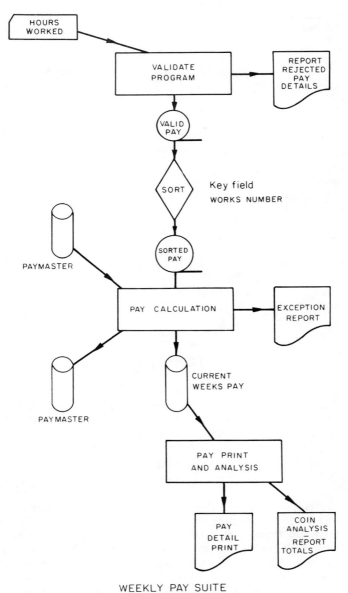

WEEKLY PAY SUITE

Fig. 13a

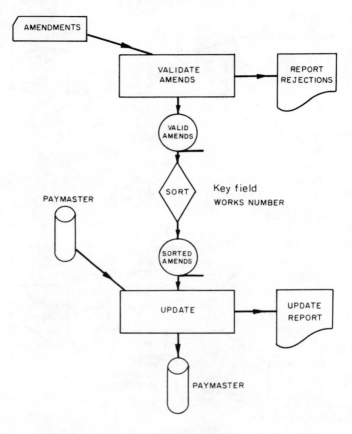

WEEKLY UPDATE SUITE

Fig. 13b

payment details on special pay slip stationery. The second report is printed at the end of the program and reports the coin analysis. This is a report of how many notes and coins of each denomination must be ordered from the bank. It also prints the totals of gross pay, net pay and the various deductions. These reports are used by the payroll clerk so that he can make up the pay for distribution on Friday morning.

This pay system describes a simple but typical batch computer system.

Real-time interactive

The speed at which the information is needed and the up-to-dateness of that information determines whether a system needs to be 'real-time'.

A real-time system can be defined as one in which the computer is used to process information and produce results in a form of data or actions in a short enough time to affect the environment in which the information originated. Real-time is not necessarily immediate, it may be 3 seconds or 30 seconds, as long as that time delay or *response* time is appropriate for the application. Booking systems and enquiry systems are the classic real-time applications. With a booking system if someone books a plane ticket they want to know if that booking is possible in a short time. A person might be prepared to wait one minute for a reply, having made the booking. The computer must update the booking information files immediately so as to prevent another enquiry taking the seat.

With an enquiry system the response time must be acceptable to the enquirer. Long response times could lead to the loss of business. Stock control systems are becoming more common as companies are needing careful monitoring of stock movement.

Let us look at a stock control system in more detail. This system is not a true real-time system; it does not affect the environment but it does keep up-to-date information. It is an interactive system.

Assume a system for a cut-price warehouse that sells direct to the customer. All stock is described and pictured in a catalogue which is readily available to the customer. Each item of stock has a unique stock number.

A customer chooses an item from the catalogue and tells the storeman the item required and the quantity. Using a video terminal, the storeman enters an order message with the order details, and the message is passed to the message module. The module validates the message for format and catalogue number errors. If the message is invalid the module displays to the screen ORDER MESSAGE INVALID, and the storeman will re-enter the order. If the order is valid the stock module is called and the stock file, which is an indexed sequential file, is accessed using the catalogue number.

The stock file contains details of quantities in stock and the bin number in which that stock is held. (A bin number is a rack reference.) If the quantity being ordered is not available the stock module will return to the message module, a message will be displayed saying STOCK NOT AVAILABLE. If the stock is available the stock file will be updated to put a hold on the stock and control will pass to the message

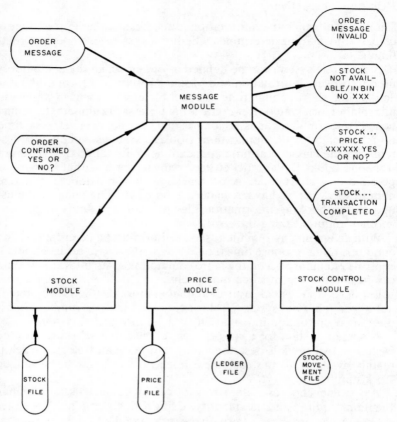

Fig. 14

module where a message STOCK XXXX QUANTITY XXX IN BIN NO XXXXX is displayed. The storeman will go to the correct bin and bring the goods for the customer's inspection. Meanwhile the price module is called and the price file, which is also indexed sequential is accessed and the price of the item and the order calculated. Control returns to the message module and the message STOCK XXXX QUANTITY XXX PRICE XXXXXX. CONFIRM ORDER YES OR NO? is displayed. If the customer does not like the goods or the displayed price, the storeman enters NO and the STOCK module is called to take the hold off the stock. If the customer wants to purchase the goods the storeman enters YES.

The stock module is called and permanently updates the stock file to reflect the selling of the item. The invoice module is called and an entry is written to the sequential ledger file with details of the transaction. The stock control module is called to write a stock movement record to a sequential file. This file contains details of every item of stock sold and will be used later for stock re-ordering and sales statistics. When all this has been done control returns to the message module and the message STOCK XXXX QUANTITY XXX TRANSACTION COMPLETED.

The ledger and stock movement files are both input to batch programs at the end of the day.

This system gives you a simplified view of what a real-time system might look like. Notice that there are four program modules permanently available and that the control program, the message module, takes one piece of data or message and calls the relevant module to process it. In this system the storeman has a video terminal with a screen and keyboard. He serves one customer at a time, but there may be many storemen each sending messages. This example of an interactive system where a person transacts a piece of business has led to naming this type of system a *transaction processing* system or TP.

The COBOL coding of a TP program is not difficult; the only difference to batch programs is the logic design. The program deals with one record at a time and starts when the first message is entered and finishes when the machine is switched off. You will notice that modules are 'called' and some of the COBOL verbs taught in chapter 12 will be used.

Appendix 1

COBOL Reserved Words

ACCEPT	CHARACTER	CURRENCY
ACCESS	CHARACTERS	DATA
ADD	CLOCK-UNITS	DATE
ADVANCING	CLOSE	DATE-COMPILED
AFTER	COBOL	DATE-WRITTEN
ALL	CODE	DAY
ALPHABETIC	CODE-SET	DEBUG-CONTENTS
ALSO	COLLATING	DEBUG-ITEM
ALTER	COLUMN	DEBUG-LINE
ALTERNATE	COMMA	DEBUG-NAME
AND	COMMUNICATION	DEBUG-SUB-1
ARE	COMP	DEBUG-SUB-2
AREA	COMPUTATIONAL	DEBUG-SUB-3
AREAS	COMP-1	DEBUGGING
ASCENDING	COMP-3	DECIMAL-POINT
ASSIGN	COMP-5	DECLARATIVES
AT	COMPUTATIONAL-1	DELETE
AUTHOR	COMPUTATIONAL-3	DELIMITED
BEFORE	COMPUTATIONAL-5	DELIMITER
BLANK	COMPUTE	DEPENDING
BLOCK	CONFIGURATION	DESCENDING
BOTTOM	CONTAINS	DESTINATION
BY	CONTROL	DETAIL
CALL	CONTROLS	DISABLE
CANCEL	COPY	DISPLAY
CD	CORR	DIVIDE
CF	CORRESPONDING	DIVISION
CH	COUNT	DOWN

DUPLICATES
DYNAMIC
EGI
ELSE
EMI
ENABLE
END-OF-PAGE
ENTER
ENVIRONMENT
EOP
EQUAL
ERROR
ESI
EVERY
EXCEPTION
EXIT
EXTEND
FILE
FILE-CONTROL
FILLER
FIRST
FOOTING
FOR
FROM
GENERATE
GIVING
GREATER
GROUP
HEADING
HIGH-VALUE
HIGH-VALUES
I-O
I-O-CONTROL
IDENTIFICATION
INDEX
INDEXED
INDICATE

INITIAL
INITIALISE
INITIALIZE
INITIATE
INPUT
INPUT—OUTPUT
INSPECT
INSTALLATION
INTO
INVALID
JUST
JUSTIFIED
KEY
LABEL
LAST
LEADING
LEFT
LENGTH
LESS
LIMIT
LIMITS
LINAGE
LINAGE-COUNTER
LINE
LINE-COUNTER
LINES
LINKAGE
LOCK
LOW-VALUE
LOW-VALUES
MEMORY
MERGE
MESSAGE
MODE
MODULES
MOVE
MULTIPLE
MULTIPLY
NATIVE
NEGATIVE
NEXT

NOT
NUMBER
NUMERIC
OBJECT-COMPUTER
OCCURS
OMITTED
OPEN
OPTIONAL
ORGANISATION
ORGANIZATION
OVERFLOW
PAGE
PAGE-COUNTER
PERFORM
PF
PH
PIC
PICTURE
PLUS
POINTER
POSITION
POSITIVE
PRINTING
PROCEDURE
PROCEDURES
PROCEED
PROGRAM
PROGRAM-ID
QUEUE
QUOTE
QUOTES
RANDOM
RD
READ
RECEIVE
RECORD
RECORDS
REDEFINES

REEL	SENTENCE	TAPE
REFERENCES	SEPARATE	TERMINAL
RELATIVE	SEQUENCE	TERMINATE
RELEASE	SEQUENTIAL	TEXT
REMAINDER	SET	THAN
REMOVAL	SIGN	THROUGH
RENAMES	SIZE	THRU
REPLACING	SORT	TIME
REPORT	SORT-MERGE	TIMES
REPORTING	SOURCE	TO
REPORTS	SOURCE-COMPUTER	TOP
RERUN	SPACE	TRAILING
RESERVE	SPACES	TYPE
RESET	SPECIAL-NAMES	UNIT
RETURN	STANDARD	UNSTRING
REVERSED	STANDARD-1	UNTIL
REWIND	START	UP
REWRITE	STATUS	UPON
RF	STOP	USAGE
RH	STRING	USE
RIGHT	SUB-QUEUE-1	USING
ROUNDED	SUB-QUEUE-2	VALUE
RUN	SUB-QUEUE-3	VALUES
SAME	SUBTRACT	VARYING
SD	SUM	WHEN
SEARCH	SUPPRESS	WITH
SECTION	SYMBOLIC	WORDS
SECURITY	SYNC	WORKING-STORAGE
SEGMENT	SYNCHRONISED	WRITE
SEGMENT-LIMIT	SYNCHRONIZED	ZERO
SELECT	TABLE	ZEROES
SEND	TALLYING	ZEROS

Appendix 2

COBOL Syntax

IDENTIFICATION DIVISION

PROGRAM-ID. program-name.
[AUTHOR. comment-entry ...]
[INSTALLATION. comment-entry ...]
[DATE-WRITTEN. comment-entry ...]
[DATE-COMPILED. comment-entry ...]
[SECURITY. comment-entry ...]
ENVIRONMENT DIVISION.
CONFIGURATION SECTION.
SOURCE-COMPUTER. computer-name
OBJECT-COMPUTER. computer-name
INPUT-OUTPUT SECTION.
FILE-CONTROL.
      SELECT-sentence ...

SELECT-*sentence*
Format 1

```
    SELECT filename
    ASSIGN TO implementor-name
  [ {ORGANISATION} IS SEQUENTIAL]
    {ORGANIZATION}
    [ACCESS MODE IS SEQUENTIAL].
```

Format 2

```
    SELECT filename
    ASSIGN TO implementor-name
    {ORGANIZATION} IS INDEXED
    {ORGANISATION}

                          {SEQUENTIAL}
    [ ACCESS MODE IS {RANDOM     } ]
                          {DYNAMIC   }
    RECORD KEY is data-name.
```

```
DATA DIVISION
[FILE SECTION.
        [file-description-entry
         [record-description-entry] ...]
[WORKING-STORAGE SECTION.
        record-description-entry ...]
[LINKAGE SECTION.
        record-description-entry ...]
```

File-description-entry

```
FD filename
[RECORDING MODE IS mode-name]
[BLOCK CONTAINS [integer-1 TO] integer-2 {RECORDS   }]
                                         {CHARACTERS}
[RECORD CONTAINS [integer-3 TO] integer-4 CHARACTERS]
[LABEL              {STANDARD}]
                    {OMITTED }
[VALUE OF implementor-name IS {data-name-1} ]
                              {literal-1  }
[DATA {RECORD IS  } data-name-2 [data-name-3] ]...
      {RECORDS ARE}
```

Record-description-entry

Format 1

```
level-number {data-name-1}
             {FILLER     }
    [REDEFINES data-name-2]
    {PICTURE} IS character-string
    {PIC    }
                  {COMPUTATIONAL   }
                  {COMP            }
                  {COMPUTATIONAL-3 }
                  {COMP-3          }
    [USAGE IS]    {COMPUTATIONAL-5 }
                  {COMP-5          }
                  {DISPLAY         }
OCCURS integer-1
    {TIMES                                              }
    {TO integer-2 TIMES DEPENDING ON data-name-3}
    [INDEXED BY index-name-1 [index-name-2] ...]]
  {SYNCHRONIZED}
  {SYNCHRONISED} RIGHT
  {SYNC        }
[VALUE IS literal-1].
```

Format 2

```
88 condition-name  ⎰VALUE IS  ⎱
                   ⎱VALUES ARE⎰ literal-1
[THRU        literal-2]
[literal-3 [THRU          literal-4]] ... .
```

PROCEDURE DIVISION

```
[USING identifier-1 [identifier-2] ...].
```

Conditions

Relation condition

```
                               ⎧IS [NOT] GREATER THAN⎫
                               ⎪IS [NOT] >           ⎪
⎧identifier-1             ⎫    ⎪IS [NOT] LESS THAN   ⎪
⎨literal-1                ⎬    ⎨IS [NOT] <           ⎬
⎩arithmetic-expression-1 ⎭    ⎪IS [NOT] EQUAL TO    ⎪
                               ⎩IS [NOT] =           ⎭

                               ⎧identifier-2             ⎫
                               ⎨literal-2                ⎬
                               ⎩arithmetic-expression-2. ⎭
```

Class condition

```
identifier IS [NOT] ⎧NUMERIC     ⎫
                    ⎨ALPHABETIC  ⎬
                    ⎩ALPHABETIC-1⎭
```

Condition-name condition

```
[NOT] condition-name
```

Sign condition

```
⎧identifier            ⎫            ⎧POSITIVE⎫
⎨arithmetic-expression ⎬ IS [NOT]  ⎨NEGATIVE⎬
⎩                      ⎭            ⎩ZERO    ⎭
```

Compound conditions

```
condition ⎧AND⎫ condition [ ⎧AND⎫condition ]...
          ⎩OR ⎭            ⎩OR ⎭
```

ACCEPT *statement*

```
ACCEPT identifier
```

ADD *statement*

Format 1

```
ADD {literal-1   } [literal-2   ] ... TO identifier-m
    {identifier-1} [identifier-2]
[ROUNDED] [identifier-n [ROUNDED]]...
```

Format 2

```
ADD {literal-1   } {literal-2   } [literal-3   ] ...
    {identifier-1} {identifier-2} [identifier-3]
    GIVING identifier-m [ROUNDED] [identifier-n [ROUNDED]]...

CALL [language-name] literal-1
     [USING identifier-1] ...
CLOSE filename-1 ...
COMPUTE identifier-1
     [ROUNDED] [identifier-2] ...
{FROM  }
{=     }arithmetic-expression
{EQUALS}
COPY text-name
DELETE filename RECORD
     INVALID KEY imperative-statement
DISPLAY {literal   } ...
        {identifier}
```

DIVIDE *statement*

Format 1

```
DIVIDE {identifier-1} INTO identifier-2
       {literal-1   }
[ROUNDED] [identifier-3 [ROUNDED]] ...
```

Format 2

```
DIVIDE {identifier-1} INTO {identifier-2}
       {literal-1   }      {literal-2   }
GIVING identifier-3
[ROUNDED] [identifier-4 [ROUNDED]]...
```

Format 3

```
DIVIDE {identifier-1} INTO {identifier-2}
       {literal-1   }      {literal-2   }
GIVING identifier-3
[ROUNDED]
REMAINDER identifier-4
```

EXIT [PROGRAM].

GO TO *statement*

Format 1

    <u>GO</u> TO procedure-name-1

Format 2

    <u>GO</u> TO procedure-name-1
    [procedure-name-2] ... procedure-name-n
    <u>DEPENDING</u> ON identifier

IF *statement*

<u>IF</u> condition {sequence of statements / <u>NEXT SENTENCE</u>} [<u>ELSE</u> {sequence of statements / <u>NEXT SENTENCE</u>}]

{<u>INITIALIZE</u> / <u>INITIALISE</u>} identifier-1 [identifier-2] ...

INSPECT *statement*

Format 1

    <u>INSPECT</u> identifier-1
    <u>TALLYING</u> identifier-2 <u>FOR</u> { {<u>ALL</u> / <u>LEADING</u>} {literal-1 / identifier-3} / <u>CHARACTERS</u> }
    [{<u>BEFORE</u> / <u>AFTER</u>} INITIAL {literal-2 / identifier-4}] ...

Format 2

    <u>INSPECT</u> identifier
                    <u>CHARACTERS</u> <u>BY</u> {literal-4 / identifier-6}
        <u>REPLACING</u> { {<u>ALL</u> / <u>LEADING</u> / <u>FIRST</u>} {literal-3 / identifier-5} <u>BY</u> {literal-4 / identifier-6} }
    [{<u>BEFORE</u> / <u>AFTER</u>} INITIAL {literal-5 / identifier-7}]

<u>MOVE</u> {identifier-1 / literal-1} <u>TO</u> identifier-2 [identifier-3]...

MULTIPLY *statement*

Format 1

    <u>MULTIPLY</u> {identifier-1 / literal-1} <u>BY</u> identifier-2
    [<u>ROUNDED</u>] [identifier-3 [<u>ROUNDED</u>]] ...

Format 2

```
MULTIPLY {identifier-1} BY {identifier-2}
         {literal-1   }    {literal-2   }
   GIVING identifier-3
   [ROUNDED] [identifier-4 [ROUNDED]] ...
OPEN {INPUT } filename-1 ...
     {OUTPUT}
     {I-O   }
```

PERFORM *statement*

Format 1

```
    PERFORM procedure-name-1
[  {THRU    } procedure-name-2]
   {THROUGH }
```

Format 2

```
    PERFORM procedure-name-1
[  {THRU    } procedure-name-2]
   {THROUGH }
   {identifier-1} TIMES
   {integer-1   }
```

Format 3

```
    PERFORM procedure-name-1
[  {THRU    } procedure-name-2]
   {THROUGH }
   UNTIL condition-1
```

Format 4

```
    PERFORM procedure-name-1
[  {THRU    } procedure-name-2]
   {THROUGH }
   VARYING {identifier-1} FROM {identifier-2}
           {index-name-1}      {index-name-2}
                               {literal-1   }
   BY {identifier-3} UNTIL condition-1
      {literal-2   }
```

READ *statement*

Format 1

```
   READ filename RECORD
   [INTO identifier]
   AT END imperative-statement
```

Format 2

```
READ filename RECORD
[INTO identifier]
INVALID KEY imperative-statement
```

REWRITE *statement*

```
REWRITE record-name [FROM identifier]
  INVALID KEY imperative-statement
```

SEARCH-*statement*

```
SEARCH identifier-1
  [AT END imperative statement-1]
  WHEN condition-1 {imperative-statement-2 }...
                   {NEXT SENTENCE
```

SET *statement*

Format 1

```
SET {index-name-1} {index-name 2} ... TO {index-name-3 }
    {identifier-1} {identifier-2}        {identifier-3 }
                                         {integer-1    }
```

Format 2

```
SET index-name-4 [index-name-5] ...
{UP BY  } {identifier-4 }
{DOWN BY} {integer-1    }
```

START *statement*

```
START filename
  KEY {IS GREATER THAN } data-name
      {IS =            }
      {IS NOT <        }
      {IS >            }
  INVALID KEY imperative-statement
```

STRING *statement*

```
STRING {identifier-1 } [identifier-2 ]
       {literal-1    } [literal-2    ] ...
            DELIMITED BY     {identifier-3 }
                             {literal-3    }
                             {SIZE         }
       [ {identifier-4 } [identifier-5 ]
         {literal-4    } [literal-5    ] ...
              DELIMITED BY {identifier-6 } ]
                           {literal-6    }  '...
                           {SIZE         }

    INTO identifier-7
```

SUBTRACT *statement*

Format 1

```
SUBTRACT {literal-1  } [literal-2  ]
         {identifier-1} [identifier-2] ...
FROM identifier-m
[ROUNDED] [identifier-n [ROUNDED]] ...
```

Format 2

```
SUBTRACT {literal-1  } [literal-2  ]
         {identifier-1} [identifier-2] ...
FROM {literal-m    } GIVING identifier-n
     {identifier-m }
[ROUNDED] [identifier-o [ROUNDED]] ...
```

UNSTRING *statement*

```
UNSTRING identifier-1
[DELIMITED BY                 {identifier-2 }
                              {literal-1    }

      OR           {identifier-3 } ]
                   {literal-2     }   ...
      INTO identifier-4 [identifier-5]...
```

WRITE *statement*

Format 1

```
WRITE record-name
[FROM identifier-1]
[ {BEFORE} ADVANCING { {identifier-2} } [LINES] } ]
  {AFTER.}           { {integer     }         }
                     {  PAGE        }
```

Format 2

```
WRITE record-name [FROM identifier-1]
INVALID KEY imperative-statement
```

Appendix 3

The Collating-Sequence

In chapter 5 we saw how characters were held in a byte. A byte has 8 bits and there are 256 possible combinations of bit patterns. We saw that this complex bit pattern can be more simply described using the EBCDIC notation. EBCDIC is an acronym for Extended Binary Coded Decimal Interchange Code. Each quartet or 4 bit group could be described as holding a value from 0 to 15 or 0 to F in EBCDIC.

The following table describes the EBCDIC and the decimal value for each bit pattern held in a byte. The third column is the character which will be printed for that bit pattern. The EBCDIC for some of the special characters can vary between computer manufacturers. The alphabetic and numeric characters are consistent between manufacturers. Notice that there are many EBCDIC values without an assigned character. The Null value is the lowest value and can be described as LOW-VALUES in COBOL. The Eight Ones is the highest value and can be described as HIGH-VALUES in COBOL.

When comparing two values the machine uses the decimal value to decide which is the greater. This is why this table is called the Collating-Sequence. This table describes the characters that can be represented by the computer and may also be known as the Character Set.

The important and most commonly used characters are space, full stop, A through Z and 0 through 9. Some other special characters, such as = ,) and (are also widely used. It is useful to memorise the order, within the collating-sequence of the following common characters.

space
A through Z
0 through 9

In other words space is before letters and numbers and letters are
before numbers. This may not be what you would expect.

The collating-sequence

EBCDIC

Hexadecimal	Decimal	Character
00	0	NULL
01	1	Start of Heading (TC1)
02	2	Start of Text (TC2)
03	3	End of Text (TC3)
04	4	
05	5	Horizontal Tabulate (FE1)
06	6	
07	7	DELete
08	8	
09	9	
0A	10	
0B	11	Vertical Tabulate (FE3)
0C	12	Form Feed (FE4)
0D	13	Carriage Return (FE5)
0E	14	Shift Out
0F	15	Shift In
10	16	Data Link Escape (TC7)
11	17	Device Control 1
12	18	Device Control 2
13	19	Device Control 3
14	20	
15	21	New Line
16	22	Back Space (FE0)
17	23	
18	24	CANcel
19	25	End of Medium
1A	26	
1B	27	
1C	28	IS4 (File Separator)
1D	29	IS3 (Group Separator)
1E	30	IS2 (Record Separator)
1F	31	IS1 (Unit Separator)
20	32	Multiple SPace
21	33	Multiple New Line
22	34	Vertical Position

EBCDIC

Hexadecimal	Decimal	Character
23	35	
24	36	
25	37	Line Feed (FE2)
26	38	End of Transmission Block (TC10)
27	39	ESCape
28	40	
29	41	
2A	42	
2B	43	
2C	44	
2D	45	ENQuiry (TC5)
2E	46	ACKnowledge (TC6)
2F	47	BELL
30	48	
31	49	
32	50	SYNchronous idle (TC9)
33	51	
34	52	
35	53	
36	54	
37	55	End of Transmission (TC4)
38	56	
39	57	
3A	58	
3B	59	
3C	60	Device Control 4
3D	61	Negative AcKnowledge (TC8)
3E	62	
3F	63	SUBstitute
40	64	SPace
41	65	
42	66	
43	67	
44	68	
45	69	
46	70	
47	71	
48	72	
49	73	

EBCDIC

Hexadecimal	Decimal	Character
4A	74	[(left bracket)
4B	75	. (fullstop)
4C	76	< (less than)
4D	77	((left parenthesis)
4E	78	+ (plus)
4F	79	! (exclamation mark)
50	80	& (ampersand)
51	81	
52	82	
53	83	
54	84	
55	85	
56	86	
57	87	
58	88	
59	89	
5A	90	] (right bracket)
5B	91	$ (dollar)
5C	92	* (asterisk)
5D	93	) (right parenthesis)
5E	94	; (semicolon)
5F	95	^ (circumflex)
60	96	− (minus)
61	97	/ (solidus)
62	98	
63	99	
64	100	
65	101	
66	102	
67	103	
68	104	
69	105	| (vertical bar)
6A	106	⦙ (broken vertical bar)
6B	107	, (comma)
6C	108	% (percentage)
6D	109	− (underline)
6E	110	> (greater than)
6F	111	? (question mark)
70	112	
71	113	

EBCDIC

Hexadecimal	Decimal	Character
72	114	
73	115	
74	116	
75	117	
76	118	
77	119	
78	120	
79	121	` (grave)
7A	122	: (colon)
7B	123	£ (pound)
7C	124	@ (at)
7D	125	´ (apostrophe, acute)
7E	126	= (equal)
7F	127	" (double quote)
80	128	
81	129	a
82	130	b
83	131	c
84	132	d
85	133	e
86	134	f
87	135	g
88	136	h
89	137	i
8A	138	
8B	139	
8C	140	
8D	141	
8E	142	
8F	143	
90	144	
91	145	j
92	146	k
93	147	l
94	148	m
95	149	n
96	150	o
97	151	p
98	152	q
99	153	r

EBCDIC

Hexadecimal	Decimal	Character
9A	154	
9B	155	
9C	156	
9D	157	
9E	158	
9F	159	
A0	160	
A1	161	˜ (tilde)
A2	162	s
A3	163	t
A4	164	u
A5	165	v
A6	166	w
A7	167	x
A8	168	y
A9	169	z
AA	170	
AB	171	
AC	172	
AD	173	
AE	174	
AF	175	
B0	176	
B1	177	
B2	178	
B3	179	
B4	180	
B5	181	
B6	182	
B7	183	
B8	184	
B9	185	
BA	186	
BB	187	
BC	188	
BD	189	
BE	190	
BF	191	
C0	192	{ (left brace)
C1	193	A

EBCDIC

Hexadecimal	*Decimal*	*Character*
C2	194	B
C3	195	C
C4	196	D
C5	197	E
C6	198	F
C7	199	G
C8	200	H
C9	201	I
CA	202	
CB	203	
CC	204	Prefix code
CD	205	
CE	206	
CF	207	
D0	208	} (right brace)
D1	209	J
D2	210	K
D3	211	L
D4	212	M
D5	213	N
D6	214	O
D7	215	P
D8	216	Q
D9	217	R
DA	218	
DB	219	
DC	220	
DD	221	
DE	222	
DF	223	
E0	224	\ (reverse solidus)
E1	225	
E2	226	S
E3	227	T
E4	228	U
E5	229	V
E6	230	W
E7	231	X
E8	232	Y
E9	233	Z

EBCDIC

Hexadecimal	Decimal	Character
EA	234	
EB	235	
EC	236	
ED	237	
EE	238	
EF	239	
F0	240	0 Zero
F1	241	1
F2	242	2
F3	243	3
F4	244	4
F5	245	5
F6	246	6
F7	247	7
F8	248	8
F9	249	9
FA	250	
FB	251	
FC	252	
FD	253	
FE	254	
FF	255	Eight ones

Appendix 4

Exercise Solutions

Simple program quiz solution (p. 33)

1 An asterisk (*).
2 PROGRAM–ID.
3 CONFIGURATION SECTION.
4 A line printer.
5 There should be a space, MS MS01.
6 (a) There should be a hyphen in FILE–CONTROL.
  (b) SELECT not SELECTED.
  (c) FILE is a reserved word.
  (d) Full stop missing.
7 (a) Level number 00 is invalid.
  (b) 9 and X cannot appear in the same PICTURE clause.
  (c) PICTURE missing for WS–TYPE, or wrong level number for WS–PART.
  (d) WS–PART is not a unique data-name.
  (e) Level number 50 is invalid, missing closed bracket after 20.
8 Figurative-constants.
9 (a) 0714
  (b) ORAN
10 INPUT, OUTPUT, I–O.
11 The record buffer.
12 (a) 469
  (b) 947
13 STOP RUN.
14 Area A.
15 (a) Elementary
  (b) Group
  (c) Group

Data division solutions (p. 43)

1 (a) v is not valid in non-numeric fields.
  (b) COMP SYNC RIGHT can only be used with numeric fields.
  (c) s is not valid in non-numeric fields.
  (d) COUNT is a reserved word.
  (e) PIC 1 must have a usage COMP–5.
  (f) COMP–9 is not a valid usage.
  (g) A full stop must complete a statement.
  (h) Non-numeric literals must have quotes.
  (i) Negative value not allowed with unsigned field.
  (j) Value too large for the picture.
  (k) v is not valid in a numeric value; full stop should be used.
  (l) Picture clause is not allowed at group level.

2 (a) 07 WS-NUM   PIC 9(7).
  (b) 03 WS-DEC   PIC 9(4)V99.
  (c) 01 WS-NAME   PIC X(20).
  (d) 05 WS-BIT   PIC S1(3) COMP-5.
  (e) 01 WS-BIN   PIC 9(4) COMP SYNC RIGHT.
  (f) 03 WS-PACK   PIC S9(5) COMP-3.

3 (a) PIC X(10) VALUE "REPORT".
  (b) PIC 9(5) COMP-3 VALUE 123.
  (c) PIC 9(3)V99 VALUE 23.5.
  (d) PIC X(10) VALUE "△△△△△DAY".
  (e) PIC 9(6) COMP SYNC RIGHT VALUE ZEROS.
  (f) PIC X(7) VALUE "*******".
  (g) PIC 1(2) COMP-5 VALUE 3.

4 01 DA-REC.
      03 DA-TYPE   PIC X.
      03 DA-GROUP.
          05 DA-AREA   PIC A(5).
          05 DA-CODE   PIC 9(4).
      03 DA-AMOUNT   PIC S9(4)V99.
      03 DA-COST   PIC 9(6) COMP SYNC RIGHT.

5 01 DA-REC.
      03 DA-TYPE   PIC X.
      03 FILLER   PIC XXX.
      03 DA-GROUP.
          05 FILLER   PIC A(5).
          05 DA-CODE   PIC 9(4).
      03 DA-AMOUNT   PIC 9(7) COMP-3.

6   03 A-FIELD   PIC 9(8).
      03 A-FIELD-AGAIN   REDEFINES A-FIELD
                             PIC X(8).

7 (a) 0100   0000
  (b) 1111   0110

   (c) 1100   0010
   (d) 0101   1011

8 (a) 10
   (b) E7
   (c) AD
   (d) 83

9 (a) space
   (b) C
   (c) minus (−)
   (d) full stop (.)
   (e) 2

Data manipulation and arithmetic solutions (p. 52)

1 (a) 613
   (b) 004987
   (c) 0125
   (d) 001278
   (e) ABCΔΔ
   (f) 1234AB

2 (a) A-NUM = 13   B-NUM = 24
   (b) A-NUM = 100   B-NUM = 120
   (c) A-NUM = 26   B-NUM = 39.5
   (d) A-NUM = 60   B-NUM = 060
   (e) A-NUM = 12.5 B-NUM = 27.7   C-NUM = 015
   (f) A-NUM = 320
   (g) A-NUM = 70   B-NUM = 00
   (h) A-NUM = 1.35 B-NUM = 009.5
   (i) A-NUM = 03
   (j) A-NUM = 100   B-NUM = 08   C-NUM = 04

3 MULTIPLY HOUR-RATE BY HOURS
       GIVING NET-PAY.
   MULTIPLY NET-PAY BY 30 GIVING
       WORK-AREA.
   DIVIDE 100 INTO WORK-AREA.
   SUBTRACT WORK-AREA FROM NET-PAY.
   SUBTRACT INSURE FROM NET-PAY.
   ADD BONUS TO NET-PAY.

4 (a) COMPUTE X-NUM = A-NUM / B-NUM + C-NUM − 70.
   (b) COMPUTE X-NUM = A-NUM * 60 / B-NUM.

Sequence control solutions (p. 69)

1 (a) YES
  (b) YES
  (c) YES
  (d) NO

2 IF IN-ACCOUNT NUMERIC AND
       IN-ACCOUNT > 110
       GO TO PARA-VALID.

3 IF IN-CODE = 3   IF IN-CODE = 3
     GO TO A-PARA   or   GO TO A-PARA.
     ELSE   ADD 1 TO IN-COUNT.
     ADD 1 TO IN-COUNT.

4 IF IN-NUM NEGATIVE
       ADD 10 TO IN-TOTAL
       MOVE ZERO TO IN-PART.

5   03 IN-AGE   PIC 99.
         88 MINOR   VALUE 0 THRU 17.
         88 ADULT   VALUE 18.
         88 PENSIONER   VALUE 65.

6 (a) A paragraph name must follow a section name.
  (b) GO TO THE–END. The word SECTION is incorrect.
  (c) OUTPUT is a reserved word and not allowed as a paragraph-
      name.
  (d) END PARA is not a valid paragraph name, END–PARA is
      correct.

7 (a) Correct
  (b) Incorrect PARA–D follows PARA–A.
  (c) Incorrect, PERFORM SECT2, would be correct.

8   IF A-COLOUR = "GREEN" AND
           A-SIZE > 3
                   MOVE A-TYPE TO B-TYPE
                   ADD A-NUM TO WS-TOTAL
                   GO TO M-PARA.
       MOVE A-NUM TO C-NUM.
       IF A-PAPER ALPHABETIC OR
          A-QTY POSITIVE
                   PERFORM PAPER-PARA.
   M-PARA.

9 CC-VALIDATE.
       IF IN-TYPE = "EF" OR
          IN-TYPE = "XY" NEXT SENTENCE
       ELSE
           GO TO ZZ-INVALID.
       IF IN-AMOUNT NUMERIC AND
          IN-AMOUNT POSITIVE NEXT SENTENCE

```
    ELSE
        GO TO ZZ-INVALID.
    IF IN-QTY NUMERIC AND
        IN-QTY > 10 NEXT SENTENCE
    ELSE
        GO TO ZZ-INVALID.
    IF IN-CODE < "0" OR
        IN-CODE > "4" GO TO ZZ-INVALID.
    GO TO AA-VALID.
```

Sequential file handling solutions (p. 85)

1 (a) You cannot read an output file.
  (b) You cannot write an input file.
  (c) You cannot read a record-name only a file-name.

```
2 FD MAT-FILE.
  01 REC-1.
     03 REC-TYPE            PIC X.
     03 REC-AREA            PIC X(20).
     03 REC-NUM             PIC 999 COMP-3.

  01 REC-2.
     03 FILLER              PIC X(21).
     03 REC-ACCOUNT         PIC 9(6).
```

Record type and area are common to both records.

```
  01 REC-3.
     03 FILLER              PIC X.
     03 REC-ADDR            PIC X(60).
```

Record type is common on all three records.

```
3 WRITE REC-1.
  WRITE REC-2.
  WRITE REC-3.

4 IDENTIFICATION DIVISION.
  PROGRAM-ID. EX01.
  ENVIRONMENT DIVISION.
  CONFIGURATION SECTION.
  SOURCE-COMPUTER. ICL-2972.
  OBJECT-COMPUTER. ICL-2972.
  INPUT-OUTPUT SECTION.
  FILE-CONTROL.
      SELECT IN-FILE ASSIGN TO MT MT01.
      SELECT OUT-FILE-1 ASSIGN TO MS DA02.
      SELECT OUT-FILE-2 ASSIGN TO MS DA03.
  DATA DIVISION.
  FILE SECTION.
  FD IN-FILE.
```

```
01 IN-REC.
     03 IN-PERS              PIC 9(6).
     03 IN-NAME              PIC X(20).
     03 IN-GROUP.
         05 IN-DEPT          PIC 99.
         05 IN-UNIT          PIC 99.
         05 IN-YRS           PIC 99.
     03 IN-JOINED.
         05 IN-YEAR          PIC 99.
         05 FILLER           PIC X(4).
     03 IN-GRADE             PIC X(3).
FD OUT-FILE-1.
01 OUT-REC-1.
     03 OUT-PERS-1           PIC 9(6).
     03 OUT-NAME             PIC X(20).
     03 OUT-GRADE            PIC X(3).
     03 OUT-YEAR             PIC 99.
FD OUT-FILE-2.
01 OUT-REC-2.
     03 OUT-PERS-2           PIC 9(6).
     03 OUT-GROUP            PIC X(6).
WORKING-STORAGE SECTION.
01 WS-IN-COUNT              PIC 9(8) COMP SYNC RIGHT.
01 WS-OUT-COUNT             PIC 9(8) COMP SYNC RIGHT.
PROCEDURE DIVISION.
AA-START.
     OPEN INPUT IN-FILE.
     OPEN OUTPUT OUT-FILE-1 OUT-FILE-2.
     MOVE ZEROS TO WS-IN-COUNT WS-OUT-COUNT.
BB-READ.
     READ IN-FILE AT END GO TO CC-END.
     ADD 1 TO WS-IN-COUNT.
     MOVE IN-PERS TO OUT-PERS-1 OUT-PERS-2.
     MOVE IN-NAME TO OUT-NAME.
     MOVE IN-GROUP TO OUT-GROUP.
     MOVE IN-GRADE TO OUT-GRADE.
     MOVE IN-YEAR TO OUT-YEAR.
     WRITE OUT-REC-1.
     WRITE OUT-REC-2.
     ADD 1 TO WS-OUT-COUNT.
     GO TO BB-READ.
CC-END.
     CLOSE IN-FILE OUT-FILE-1 OUT-FILE-2.
     STOP RUN.
*    THIS SOLUTION DEMONSTRATES THE USE OF MULTIPLE
*    RECEIVING FIELDS WITH THE MOVE.
*    YOU CAN OPEN MORE THAN ONE FILE IN AN OPEN STATEMENT
*    MOVE DATA TO BOTH RECORD BUFFERS, WHEN COMPLETE
*    WRITE TO BOTH FILES SEPARATELY.
```

Table handling solutions (p. 95)

```
1 (a)  03 WS-TAB1            PIC 9(3) OCCURS 20.
  (b)  03 WS-TAB2            OCCURS 40.
           05 WS-NAM         PIC X(20).
           05 WS-ADD         PIC X(60).
  (c)  03 WS-TAB3            PIC A(4) OCCURS 10.
       03 WS-TAB4            PIC 9(6) COMP-3 OCCURS 10.
  (d)  03 WS-TAB5            PIC 9(3) OCCURS 20 TO 100
                        DEPENDING ON WS-COUNT.

2 (a) PERFORM PARA-A THRU PARA-B
          6 TIMES.
  (b) MOVE ZERO TO A-COUNT.
      PERFORM PARA-A THRU PARA-B
            UNTIL A-COUNT = 6.

3     PERFORM ADD-PARA
      VARYING SUB-AMT
        FROM 1 BY 1
            UNTIL SUB-AMT > 70.
              .
              .
              .
      ADD-PARA.
          ADD TAB-AMOUNT (SUB-AMT) TO TOTAL-AMOUNT.

4  01 WS-BANK.
       03 WS-BRANCH          OCCURS 50.
          05 WS-MANAGER      OCCURS 2.
              07 WS-STAFF PIC 9(6) COMP SYNC RIGHT OCCURS 4.

5         MOVE 20 TO A-SUB.
      PARA.
          ADD A-COUNT (A-SUB) TO TOTAL.
          MOVE A-COUNT (A-SUB) TO PR-A.
          IF A-SUB = 31
                  NEXT SENTENCE
          ELSE
              ADD 1 TO A-SUB
              GO TO PARA.
      or
          MOVE 19 TO A-SUB.
      PARA.
          ADD 1 TO A-SUB.
          ADD A-COUNT (A-SUB) TO TOTAL.
          MOVE A-COUNT (A-SUB) TO PR-A.
          IF A-SUB < 31
                  GO TO PARA.

6 IDENTIFICATION DIVISION.
  PROGRAM-ID. EX02.
  ENVIRONMENT DIVISION.
  CONFIGURATION SECTION.
  SOURCE-COMPUTER. ICL-2972.
```

```
OBJECT-COMPUTER. ICL-2972.
INPUT-OUTPUT SECTION.
FILE-CONTROL.
     SELECT IN-FILE ASSIGN TO MT MTO1.
     SELECT OUT-FILE ASSIGN TO MT MTO2.
DATA DIVISION.
FD IN-FILE.
01 IN-REC.
     03 IN-NAME                          PIC X(11).
     03 FILLER OCCURS 10.
        05 FILLER                        PIC XX.
        05 IN-VALUE                      PIC 9(8) COMP SYNC RIGHT.
*      FILLER CAN BE USED FOR ANY FIELD
*      THAT IS NOT REFERENCED IN THE PROGRAM
FD OUT-FILE.
01 OUT-REC.
     03 OUT-TYPE             PIC X.
     03 OUT-NAME             PIC X(11).
     03 OUT-VALUE            PIC 9(10) COMP SYNC RIGHT.
WORKING-STORAGE SECTION.
01 WS-SUB                    PIC 99 COMP SYNC RIGHT.
PROCEDURE DIVISION.
AA-START.
     OPEN INPUT IN-FILE.
     OPEN OUTPUT OUT-FILE.
BB-READ.
     READ IN-FILE AT END GO TO ZZ-END.
     MOVE "A" TO OUT-TYPE.
     MOVE IN-NAME TO OUT-NAME.
     MOVE ZERO TO WS-SUB OUT-VALUE.
*    THE SUBSCRIPT MUST BE SET TO ZERO
*    AT THE START OF THE LOOP.
CC-LOOP.
     ADD 1 TO WS-SUB.
     ADD IN-VALUE (WS-SUB) TO OUT-VALUE.
     IF WS-SUB = 10 NEXT SENTENCE
     ELSE GO TO CC-LOOP.
*    THE LOOP IS USED TEN TIMES FOR
*              EACH RECORD
DD-WRITE.
     WRITE OUT-REC.
     GO TO BB-READ.
*    NOTE THAT THE PROGRAM IS A LOOP,
*    YOU RETURN TO READ TO COMPLETE THE LOOP
ZZ-END.
     MOVE "Z" TO OUT-TYPE.
     MOVE SPACES TO OUT-NAME.
     MOVE ZEROS TO OUT-VALUE.
     WRITE OUT-REC.
     CLOSE IN-FILE OUT-FILE.
     STOP RUN.
*    WRITE THE FINAL RECORD AND
*    COMPLETE THE PROGRAM
```

Printing solutions (p. 106)

1 (a) FL OWE R
  (b) 21/03
  (c) 72.48
  (d) 31.82
  (e) ∆∆7431
  (f) 054.6

Note: the answer would be 546.5 if the sending field had been PIC 9(4).

  (g) ∆∆∆
  (h) 1745DB
  (i) ∆127CR
  (j) ∆317
  (k) ∆£317.50
  (l) AMERICA

2 01 WS-HEAD.
```
      03 FILLER                  PIC X(19) VALUE
      "        AREA REPORT".
      03 FILLER                  PIC X(30)    VALUE SPACES.
      03 FILLER                  PIC X(13)    VALUE
      "STATEMENT 12A".
   or
   01 WS-HEAD.                   PIC X(62) VALUE
   "         AREA REPORT                        STATEMENT 12A".
```

3 (a) WRITE PR-REC AFTER PAGE.
  (b) WRITE PR-REC AFTER 2.
  (c) WRITE PR-REC BEFORE 3.

4 (a) Incorrect. You cannot use an edited field as an arithmetic operand.
  (b) Correct.
  (c) You cannot move an edited field to a numeric field.
  (d) Correct.
  (e) Incorrect as 4(a).

5
```
IDENTIFICATION DIVISION
  PROGRAM-ID. EX03.
  ENVIRONMENT DIVISION.
  CONFIGURATION SECTION.
  SOURCE-COMPUTER. ICL-2972.
  OBJECT-COMPUTER. ICL-2972.
  INPUT-OUTPUT SECTION.
  FILE-CONTROL.
      SELECT IN-FILE ASSIGN MS DA01.
      SELECT PR-FILE ASSIGN LP LP01.
  DATA DIVISION.
  FD IN-FILE.
  01 IN-REC.
```

```
        03  IN-ACC-NUM            PIC X(6).
        03  IN-ACC-DESC           PIC X(17).
        03  IN-LIMIT              PIC 9(8) COMP SYNC RIGHT.
    FD PR-FILE.
    01 PR-REC.
        03  FILLER                PIC X(4).
        03  PR-NUM                PIC 99/9999.
        03  FILLER                PIC X(3).
        03  PR-DESC               PIC X(17).
        03  FILLER                PIC X(4).
        03  PR-LIMIT              PIC £(8)9.
    WORKING-STORAGE SECTION.
    01 WS-HEAD-1                  PIC X(50) VALUE
        "       NUMBER        DESCRIPTION              LIMIT".
    01 WS-LINE-COUNT              PIC 99 COMP SYNC RIGHT.
    PROCEDURE DIVISION.
    AA-START.
        OPEN INPUT IN-FILE.
        OPEN OUTPUT PR-FILE.
    BB-HEADING.
        MOVE ZERO TO WS-LINE-COUNT.
        MOVE SPACES TO PR-REC.
        WRITE PR-REC AFTER PAGE.
        WRITE PR-REC FROM WS-HEAD-1 AFTER 1.
        ADD 2 TO WS-LINE-COUNT.
    CC-PROCESS.
        READ IN-FILE AT END GO TO ZZ-END.
        MOVE SPACES TO PR-REC.
        MOVE IN-ACC-NUM TO PR-NUM.
        MOVE IN-ACC-DESC TO PR-DESC.
        MOVE IN-LIMIT TO PR-LIMIT.
        WRITE PR-REC AFTER 3.
        ADD 3 TO WS-LINE-COUNT.
        IF WS-LINE-COUNT = 35
            GO TO BB-HEADING.
        GO TO CC-PROCESS.
    ZZ-END.
        CLOSE IN-FILE PR-FILE.
        STOP RUN.
```

Indexed sequential solutions (p. 115)

```
1     SELECT IS-FILE ASSIGN TO MS DA03
              ORGANISATION INDEXED
              ACCESS MODE RANDOM
              RECORD KEY IS IS-KEY.
2 (a) SELECT IN-FILE ASSIGN TO MS DA05
              ORGANISATION INDEXED
              ACCESS MODE SEQUENTIAL
              RECORD KEY IS IN-KEY.
  (b) OPEN INPUT IN-FILE.
      MOVE "100" TO WS-KEY.
```

```
        START IN-FILE KEY = WS-KEY
                INVALID KEY GO TO XX-ERROR.
        READ IN-FILE AT END GO TO ZZ-END.

3  IDENTIFICATION DIVISION.
   PROGRAM-ID. EX04.
   ENVIRONMENT DIVISION.
   CONFIGURATION SECTION.
   SOURCE-COMPUTER. ICL-2972.
   OBJECT-COMPUTER. ICL-2972.
   INPUT-OUTPUT SECTION.
   FILE-CONTROL.
        SELECT CAT-FILE ASSIGN TO MT MT05.
        SELECT PRICE-FILE ASSIGN TO MS DA06
                ORGANISATION INDEXED
                ACCESS MODE RANDOM
                RECORD KEY PR-CAT-NUM.
   DATA DIVISION.
   FILE SECTION.
   FD CAT-FILE.
   01 CAT-REC.
        03 CAT-NUM            PIC X(8).
        03 FILLER             PIC X(66).
        03 CAT-QTY            PIC 9(6) COMP SYNC RIGHT.
   FD PRICE-FILE.
   01 PRICE-REC.
        03 PR-CAT-NUM         PIC X(8).
        03 PR-ITEM            PIC 9(7) COMP-3.
        03 PR-QTY-DATE        PIC 9(8) COMP SYNC RIGHT.
   WORKING-STORAGE SECTION.
   01 WS-TOT-REVENUE          PIC 9(12) COMP SYNC RIGHT.
   01 WS-ITEM-COST            PIC 9(12) COMP SYNC RIGHT.
   PROCEDURE DIVISION.
   AA-START.
        OPEN INPUT CAT-FILE.
        OPEN I-O PRICE-FILE.
        MOVE ZERO TO WS-TOT-REVENUE.
   BB-READ.
        READ CAT-FILE AT END GO TO DD-END.
        MOVE CAT-NUM TO PR-CAT-NUM.
*       MOVE THE CATALOGUE NUMBER TO THE RECORD KEY FIELD
        READ PRICE-FILE INVALID KEY GO TO BB-READ.
        ADD CAT-QTY TO PR-QTY-DATE.
        MULTIPLY PR-QTY-DATE BY PR-ITEM
                GIVING WS-ITEM-COST.
        ADD WS-ITEM-COST TO WS-TOT-REVENUE.
   CC-REWRITE.
        REWRITE PRICE-REC INVALID KEY
                GO TO BB-READ.
*       THE RECORD HAS BEEN UPDATED WITH THE
*       QUANTITY IT MUST BE REWRITTEN.
        GO TO BB-READ.
```

```
DD-END.
      DISPLAY WS-TOT-REVENUE.
      CLOSE CAT-FILE PRICE-FILE.
      STOP RUN.
```

Further procedure division solutions (p. 132)

```
1 MOVE ZERO TO WS-NUM.
  INSPECT WS-AREA
        TALLYING WS-NUM
            FOR ALL "A" BEFORE "-".
  IF WS-NUM NOT = 3
                GO TO ZZ-INVALID.

2 INSPECT WA-DESC
        REPLACING LEADING "X"
                BY SPACE.
```

Note: " " may be used instead of SPACE.

```
3 STRING BA-C DELIMITED BY SIZE
        BA-B DELIMITED BY "*"
        BA-A DELIMITED BY SIZE
  INTO    CA-AREA.

4 UNSTRING DA-NAME
        DELIMITED BY "="
  INTO FA-A FA-M FA-B FA-D.

5 SET IND-SEED TO 1.
  SEARCH WS-FLOWERS
        AT END GO TO NO-PETS
        WHEN WS-SEED (IND-SEED) = "PETUNIA"
        ADD WS-PKTS (IND-SEED) TO SEED-TOTAL.

6 ACCEPT WS-PARAM.
  DISPLAY "MESSAGE" WS-PARAM.

7 CALL COBOL "CALCPAY" USING WS-FIELD-IN
                             WS-FIELD-OUT.

8 PARA-A.
      COPY PARACOPY.
```

Index